Laura Theodore

DELICIOUSLY
Jazzy
Vegetarian's
VEGAN

Plant-Powered Recipes for the Modern, Mindful Kitchen

D1520978

Scribe Publishing Company
Royal Oak, Michigan

Scribe
(publishing)

Jazzy Vegetarian's Deliciously Vegan: Plant-Powered Recipes for the Modern, Mindful Kitchen

Published by Scribe Publishing Company
29488 Woodward, Suite 426
Royal Oak, MI 48073
www.scribe-publishing.com

Front cover photo: Laura Theodore
Interior photos and back cover food photos: Laura Theodore, Andy Ebberbach, Robert White, Julie Snyder
Back cover and back flap photos of Laura: David Kaplan
Cover and Interior Design: Miguel Camacho
Food Styling: Laura Theodore, Anne Landry
Kitchen Assistants: Tisha Christopher, Julie Snyder
Filmed at: The Drayton Mills, Spartanburg, South Carolina
Hair Styling and Make Up: Haley Parrish
Hair Design: Josh Carpenter
Dinnerware for Photos Provided by: Cardinal International

ISBN 978-0-9916021-5-5

Publisher's Cataloging-in-Publication data
Names: Theodore, Laura, author.
Title: Jazzy vegetarian's deliciously vegan : plant-powered recipes for the modern , mindful kitchen / by Laura Theodore.
Description: Includes index. | Royal Oak, MI: Scribe Publishing Company, 2018.
Identifiers: ISBN 978-0-9916021-5-5 | LCCN 2017957531
Subjects: LCSH Vegan cooking--United States. | Cooking, American. | Cookbooks. | BISAC COOKING / Vegetarian & Vegan.
Classification: LCC TX837 .T455 2018 | DDC 641.5⁄636--dc23

Jazzy Vegetarian gratefully thanks and acknowledges our Season Six Sponsor, Bertolli, whose generous support has made it possible to share these recipes with the world.

Jazzy Vegetarian gratefully acknowledges our past sponsors:

"TODAY IS THE DAY TO START LIVING MORE COMPASSIONATELY"

-Laura Theodore

PRAISE for *Jazzy Vegetarian's* DELICIOUSLY VEGAN

"Laura Theodore, the jazziest chef on the planet, offers exquisite recipes in an easy to follow format that will elevate your cooking to gourmet level. Her genius is making healthy food taste both sinful and divine."

- Jane Velez-Mitchell, NYT bestselling author/journalist, JaneUnChained.com editor

....

"I simply love Laura's delicious and very easy vegan recipes in this new book! You will never believe you're eating vegan, with dishes such as Stuffed Manicotti and Divine Chocolate Mousse Cake. Scrumptious!"

- Chloe Coscarelli, vegan chef and author

....

"Laura Theodore, the Jazzy Vegetarian, does it again with a gorgeous new cookbook filled with easy and appetizing recipes. From Cashew-Stuffed Artichokes and Garam Masala Sweet Potato Bites, to Gingered Portobello Steaks and Divine Chocolate Mousse Cake, each recipe is a winner."

- Robin Robertson, bestselling author of *Vegan Planet*, *1,000 Vegan Recipes*, *Veganize It!* and more than 20 others

....

"I'm not vegan, but the food in this book looks so gorgeously delicious that it practically jumps off the page. What I love most about Laura's cooking is her creativity. She's able to take simple ingredients and transform the way your family eats, delighting vegans and meat-lovers alike."

- Sri Rao, author of *Bollywood Kitchen*

....

"Laura Theodore's *Deliciously Vegan* is chock-full of the most inviting, heart-warming, soul-comforting meals—and they're easy and healthy to boot! This cookbook will bring joy into your kitchen and into the hearts and bellies of those you nourish."

- Ruby Roth, author-illustrator of *That's Why We Don't Eat Animals*

....

"Laura Theodore makes vegan cooking fun and accessible for everyone. The mouthwatering recipes in *Jazzy Vegetarian's Deliciously Vegan* are easy to whip up, and they'll please even the pickiest of eaters."

- Dianne Wenz, vegan health and lifestyle coach, diannesvegankitchen.com

....

"Simple elegance is what comes to mind when Laura Theodore is in the kitchen. With this new offering, Laura once again brings modern taste to the vegan table. With her easy style, she shares her bounty of scrumptious recipes that are quick to prepare, creative in design and are deliciously vegan!"

- Zsu Dever, author of *Aquafaba: Sweet and Savory Vegan Recipes Made Egg-Free with the Magic of Bean Water*

TABLE OF CONTENTS

VI

INTRODUCTION

VIII

FROM ROCK-N-ROLL *BABE* – TO PBS *CHEF*

I first saw my husband, Andy, while wailing hard-core, blues rock-riffs on the stage of the Bitter End Nightclub in New York City. My cult band "Q" was all the rage in certain circles, and we loved playing our intense, politically inspired music surrounded by the funky red brick stage backdrop and cool vibe of this notable venue.

One more detail—I *saw* my husband, but I didn't know it at the time. Ours is a beautifully romantic story, as many New York City love stories go. You see, at the time, my husband-to-be was playing guitar in another rock band. On that particular evening, his bass player suggested that they go and check out this awesome chick singer with fiery red and blonde hair who regularly blew the roof off of clubs with her powerhouse vocals. So, as I sang my heart out in front of the packed crowd, my husband said to himself that he'd like to ask me out. How *that* was going to happen remained to be seen, as we did not even meet each other that night.

Fast-forward several days. I arrived at Andy's recording studio where I was going to be recording my first album—a *jazz* record—and who opened the door but my "to-be" husband! At first he didn't realize I was the same person he had recently seen *rockin'* the house a few days before. You see, I was dressed somewhat conservatively in a pinstriped, button down shirt and jeans, with my below waist length mane tied back in a neat bun. We said our hellos, set up the session, and then I started to sing.

I started purring out velvety vocals, and all of a sudden I heard an enthusiastic voice speak over the studio talk back. "Wait a minute… weren't you the girl singing a few nights ago at the Bitter End? You were AWESOME!"

Flattered, I replied, "Yes, thanks so much."

"But that was ROCK music! Now you're singing great jazz? Wow."

It's true. I've sung just about every style of music during my extensive career. Music has been an important part of my life as far back as I can remember, and I adore singing rock, jazz, blues, popular, contemporary and even show tunes.

WHERE DOES THE *CHEF* PART COME IN?

Today, many people know me as the perky public television and PBS vegan chef *and* singer, the *Jazzy Vegetarian*. With six jazz-oriented CDs behind me, I am widely known as a jazz singer, but my musical path has been diverse. I grew up in University Heights, Ohio, a child actor who was devoted to the sights and sounds of the musical theatre. Then, at seventeen, I started singing contemporary music when I was asked to join a Rock and Roll band. Several years later, I expanded my singing talents after I moved to Boston and began to study the art of jazz singing. When I relocated to New York City, I started working in the then popular cabaret/jazz circuit, while auditioning for Broadway shows on the side. When I landed the role of rock icon Janis Joplin in a new off-Broadway revue, my musical interests, talents and goals came full circle.

But wait, you're saying, what the heck does this story have to do with plant-based cooking? Well, for me, just about everything. Along with my passion for music, I have always loved food. As a child, visiting and learning how to prepare delicious food with my Grandma Cook fascinated me (yes, *Cook* was actually her last name), and eating my mom's tasty dinners every night was something I looked forward to. At nineteen, I moved from Ohio to Colorado, and knowing my interest in food and cooking, my grandmother regularly sent me family recipes, neatly written in her own hand on pretty recipe cards. My mother started doing the same, and soon I had compiled a comprehensive collection of family-inspired culinary delights.

As the years passed, my musical career expanded, and that's when I ended up in New York City. It was there that I continued to develop my own unique style of classic cooking, based on family recipes. Along the way, I had become interested in the idea of becoming a vegetarian and eventually a vegan. Back then there was a scarcity of tempting vegetarian or vegan recipes, so I began creating my own crowd-pleasing, plant-based dishes. I started hosting fabulous dinner soirées for my fellow musicians, friends and family, making sure to play festive music in the background throughout the meal. Music, in my opinion, is an important part of any party. After all, serving delicious food is the center of any successful get-together, but music brings *life* to the party!

FOOD AND MUSIC GO TOGETHER (LIKE PEAS IN A PLANT-BASED POD)

Think about it: music and food go together wherever we dine. Whether we're eating in a local coffee shop, dining at a five-star restaurant, grabbing a bite from a fast food joint, picking up a quick meal at a shopping mall, splashing at a pool party, sharing a casual supper with friends or hosting an elegant dinner party, music is ever-present in the background, complementing the menu while setting the mood for the meal. So that is where the *jazzy* part of the Jazzy Vegetarian comes in!

The other factor that goes hand-in-hand with my story is my life-long love for animals. Over the past ten years, I have made it my number one mission to help educate others about the shocking details of our modern day animal factory farming system by doing what I do best: pairing sassy singing with delicious, compassionate cooking!

So in the pages of this book, I'm kicking it up a notch by sharing my *jazzylicious*, plant-based recipes meant to fulfill your cravings for food that is absolutely delicious while being healthy, compassionate and environmentally friendly, and it's all easily prepared in your own home kitchen.

Thank you for joining me on my ever-evolving life journey. Now, let's get ready to cook!

XI

CHAPTER ONE
Favorite Fundamentals

I believe that eating "animal-free" is healthier for us, the planet and, of course, the animals. That's why I love sharing delicious vegan recipes, mindful food philosophies and festive menu plans with the world. My award-winning television series, *Jazzy Vegetarian*, is geared toward making vegan cooking accessible, appealing and easier for home cooks across America and beyond. *Meat Free Mondays* are becoming more popular, and home cooks are seeking to serve at least one plant-based meal each week, while adding more vegan recipes to their weekly menu plan overall.

In this chapter I'll share my top tips, along with basic ingredients to keep in your kitchen.

Laura's Top Ten Lists

LAURA'S TOP TEN
ESSENTIAL INGREDIENTS

I am often asked: *How do I get started on a vegan diet? How do I stock my kitchen?* Having the right pantry items on hand makes the journey toward preparing mindful vegan meals less daunting and easier. I have a short list of ingredients that I try to keep available so I can whip up plant-based recipes to please the palates of my family and friends.

This list can be used as a guideline to create your own "top ten" list, adding or omitting items based on your family's food preferences, sensitivities or allergies. Here are my top ten favorite plant-based essentials that I like to have stocked in my kitchen.

1. **Canned beans (black, kidney, white, pinto and garbanzo):** Canned beans make a great base for creating quick, hearty, nutrient-dense, protein *and* fiber rich vegan meals. Beans are inexpensive and extremely versatile. I use canned beans for dips, vegan burgers, burritos, soups, casseroles, salads, plant-based "cheese," appetizers and so much more. Canned beans are great for supplying great taste, good nutrition and easy convenience to your weekly menu plan. Look to purchase organic beans packed in cans made with BPA-free lining. Refrigerate canned beans after opening.

2. **Extra-virgin olive oil:** This rich and flavorful fruit oil is delicious in salad dressings, to add extra flavor to casseroles, soups, sauces or stews, as a dip for crusty bread, to lightly sauté vegetables (use medium-low heat), or to use as a substitute for butter in baked goods. The International Olive Oil Council (IOOC) defines extra-virgin olive oil as oil coming from cold pressing of the olives, containing no more than 0.8% acidity and having a superior flavor. (Note that the USDA does not regulate the labeling of IOOC produced olive oil.) Store olive oil in a dark, cool place and use within sixty days of opening.

3. **Marinara sauce (vegan) and canned tomatoes:** A good, jarred vegan marinara is my *go-to* staple for quick weeknight meals, making a time-saving base for recipes such as pasta dishes, lasagna, chili, sauces, casseroles, stews and more. I keep several jars stocked in my pantry for use when time is at a premium. Canned tomatoes provide the same flexibility for creating easy meals. I keep organic diced, crushed and fire-roasted canned tomato varieties on hand. Be sure to refrigerate marinara sauce and/or canned tomatoes after opening.

4. **Nondairy milk:** I keep aseptic packages of nondairy milk in my pantry and the refrigerated variety on hand at all times. Soy, almond, rice, oat, cashew, coconut, hemp and hazelnut nondairy milks are now readily found in both non-refrigerated packaging and in the refrigerator section of well-stocked supermarkets and health food stores. These plant-based milks make the perfect substitute for dairy milk in any recipe and can really jazz up baked goods, breakfast cereals, smoothies, vegan ice "cream," casseroles, mashed potatoes and so much more. Be sure to refrigerate the aseptic variety of nondairy milk after opening.

5. **Nuts and seeds:** In addition to being excellent sources of protein, nuts and seeds have vitamins, minerals, fiber, essential amino acids *and* healthy fats! I love to use nuts and seeds for preparing nut and seed burgers, meatless loafs, nut-"cheeze" (like *Tahini-Nut Cheeze*, page 77), nut creams and nut dressings. They also add crunch and nutrition to salads and steamed vegetables. Alone, a small handful sure makes a tasty snack! I like to use almonds, pecans, walnuts, cashews, sunflower seeds, flaxseeds and more. Flaxseeds have an impressive omega-3 fatty acid content and are high in both soluble and insoluble fiber. Right before using flaxseeds, grind them with a high-performance blending appliance, grain mill or coffee grinder that is designated for flaxseeds only, and use them right away. Their best nutritional value is released when the seeds are ground. Be sure to refrigerate nuts and seeds after opening.

6. **Grains (my favorites are brown rice, rolled oats and quinoa):** Brown rice comes in both short and long grain varieties and may be the most common grain served in vegan cooking. Brown rice has a slightly nutty flavor and is chewier than refined white rice. Brown rice is delicious cooked and then served by itself as a side dish with vegetables and beans, or as a basic ingredient in casseroles and soups. It is delightful cooked and served for breakfast with vegan milk, cinnamon and maple syrup or brown sugar. Refrigerate uncooked brown rice after purchase, as it can become rancid.

Also called old-fashioned or whole oats, rolled oats are made from the whole-grains of oats that are steamed (to make them soft and pliable), then pressed to flatten them. Rolled oats cook faster than steel-cut oats, and besides the traditional morning bowl of hearty oatmeal, I like to use rolled oats in cookies, muffins, pie crusts, crisps, quick breads, meatless loafs and vegan burgers. To make a quick, homemade oat flour, simply pour some rolled oats into a blender and process into coarse or fine flour.

With a welcoming nutty taste and packed with protein, quinoa makes an excellent alternative to brown rice. Quinoa is technically a seed (not a grain), but its texture, taste and preparation method echoes that of many whole-grains, so it is often categorized as a grain. Uncooked quinoa requires thorough rinsing but is quick to prepare and a nutritional powerhouse that is high in quality protein. I use quinoa as a main dish (cooked with canned beans), side dish or as a base for quick plant-based burgers, casseroles and salads. I suggest refrigerating grains after opening.

7. **Sweeteners (my favorites are brown sugar, cane sugar and maple syrup):** Sweeteners can add real pizzazz to vegan desserts, baked goods and sauces. Pure brown sugar is a favorite of mine because it has a distinct molasses taste that enhances many recipes, giving them a rich flavor. I use organic cane sugar when baking a cake or cookies that I want to be light in color. Please note that some sugars are filtered and bleached with bone char, which is why many refined white sugars are unsuitable for vegans. Several vegan-friendly, organic sugar companies can be found online.

For a sweet alternative, maple syrup is my go-to sweetener for salad dressings, marinara sauces, casseroles and many desserts. I use both *grade B* and *grade A* syrups. Even though *grade B* is usually slightly thicker, after many years of testing, I find them to be interchangeable in most recipes. Keep dry sugars *tightly* closed in your pantry, but be sure to refrigerate maple syrup after opening.

8. **Tamari (regular and reduced-sodium):** Tasty tamari sauce is a mainstay in my recipes. Tamari is made from soybeans with just a touch of wheat or no wheat at all. It imparts a pleasing color along with a rich, mellow taste to many savory dishes, dressings and sauces. It has a more complex flavor profile than ordinary soy sauce. Regular tamari has a concentrated, deep flavor, while the reduced-sodium version tastes lighter and has about 25 percent less sodium than regular tamari. Tamari is a great substitute for salt in many recipes. For every ¼ teaspoon of salt (about 590 mg) listed in a recipe, you may replace it with about 1 teaspoon of reduced-sodium tamari (about 233 mg). Gluten-free tamari is now readily available. Buy tamari that is MSG-free and made with non-GMO soybeans. Be sure to refrigerate tamari after opening.

9. **Tempeh and tofu:** Made from the controlled fermentation of soybeans, tempeh replaces meat in many recipes like casseroles, chili, kebabs, stir-fries and more. There are many tasty varieties available, such as five-grain or three-grain tempeh. Always buy non-GMO, organic tempeh from a reputable source. Once you get the hang of cooking with tempeh, you'll want to make it a staple in your regular diet. Be sure to always refrigerate tempeh.

   Tofu is another great source of plant-based protein. Tofu is made from soybeans, water and a coagulant. It is now widely available in supermarkets. Plain tofu comes in two main forms: regular (packed in water in refrigerated tubs and found in the refrigerated section) and silken (packed in shelf-stable aseptic cartons that must be refrigerated after opening). Each type is available in soft, firm and extra-firm varieties. Always buy non-GMO, organic tofu from a reputable source. Store any leftover tofu in the refrigerator for up to 2 days, in a tightly closed container, with fresh water to cover the tofu by ½ inch (drain and change the water each day).

10. **Whole-grain flour:** Flours made with 100 percent whole-grains are considered to have a superior nutritional profile to refined grains, offering a complex, full-bodied texture and flavor to your recipes. Look for the word "whole" on the package label. Buy certified organic flour whenever available. I love keeping whole-grain flours on hand for baking vegan quick breads, muffins and cakes. For the freshest flavor, be sure to refrigerate whole-grain flours after purchase, as they can become rancid when stored at room temperature.

6

Fabulous Flax-Oat Muffins (page 85)

LAURA'S TOP TEN
EGG SUBSTITUTIONS for BAKING

Vegan baking without the use of eggs can be tricky! When you are converting conventional baked goods recipes, sometimes a bit of experimentation is called for. Finding the right taste *and* texture to replace eggs can be challenging, so here are my top choices to use when you are creating your own egg-free, baked goods recipes.

For every egg you would like to replace with a vegan substitution, you can use:

1. ¼ cup mashed (or puréed) banana (use for a sweet taste and dense texture)

2. ¼ cup mashed (or puréed) avocado (use for a buttery taste and moist, dense texture)

3. ¼ to ⅓ cup soft, regular tofu, whipped up in the blender (use for a mild taste and dense texture)

4. ⅓ cup applesauce (use for a sweet taste and dense texture)

5. 1 tablespoon ground flaxseeds mixed with 3 tablespoons water (use for a mild taste and moist, light texture)

6. 1 teaspoon baking soda, plus 3 tablespoons lemon juice (use for a zingy taste and light texture)

7. 1 teaspoon baking soda, plus 3 tablespoons vinegar (use for a slightly acidic taste and light texture)

8. 3 tablespoons shredded, dried coconut, plus 3 tablespoons water or nondairy milk (use for a coconuty taste and dense texture)

9. 1 teaspoon baking soda, plus 2 tablespoons water, plus 1 tablespoon extra-light olive oil (use for a fruity taste and medium, moist texture)

10. If the recipe calls for only *one* egg, in most cases you can just *leave the egg out!*

LAURA'S TOP TEN
CHEESE and CREAM SAUCE SUBSTITUTIONS

Here I have made swapping out vegan versions of dairy-based cheese and cream sauces easy with these delicious, simple-to-prepare plant-based substitutes.

1. **Tangy Vegan Ricotta Cheese:** 1 block (14 to 16 ounces) firm regular tofu mashed with 1 teaspoon freshly squeezed lemon juice and ¼ teaspoon garlic powder. (Equals 14 to 16 ounces dairy ricotta cheese.)

2. **Savory Vegan Ricotta Cheese:** 1 block (14 to 16 ounces) firm tofu mashed with 1 teaspoon reduced-sodium tamari, 1 teaspoon extra-virgin olive oil and ½ teaspoon Italian seasoning blend. (Equals 14 to 16 ounces dairy ricotta cheese.)

3. **Soy-Free Vegan Ricotta Cheese:** 1 can (14 to 16 ounces) white beans (drained and rinsed), processed in the blender with ⅓ cup raw cashews and ⅓ cup water (plus more as needed). (Equals 14 to 16 ounces dairy ricotta cheese.)

4. **Vegan Feta Cheese:** 8 ounces firm regular tofu (cut into ½ to 1-inch cubes) combined with 1 tablespoon lemon juice, 1 tablespoon extra-virgin olive oil, 1 teaspoon Italian seasoning blend, ¼ teaspoon garlic powder and ¼ teaspoon salt. Cover and refrigerate for about 2 hours to allow flavors to marry. (Equals 8 ounces dairy feta cheese.)

5. **Nutty-Bean Cheese Dip:** 1 can (14 to 16 ounces) white beans (drained and rinsed), processed in the blender with ½ cup raw cashews (soaked, drained and rinsed, see note), 4 teaspoons lemon juice, 2 tablespoons water, ½ teaspoon sea salt, ⅛ to ¼ teaspoon cayenne pepper and 1 clove garlic.

CHEF'S NOTE: To soak cashews, put them in a small bowl and pour just enough water over the cashews to cover completely. Put the bowl in the refrigerator and let the cashews soak for 1 to 4 hours. Drain the cashews and rinse with cool, running water.

Seitan Fajitas with Cashew Sour "Cream" (page 198)

6. **Cauliflower "Cream" Sauce:** Cut a head of cauliflower into florets and steam until tender. Put the steamed cauliflower in a blender container and process with a bit of unsweetened nondairy milk or water until smooth, adding more nondairy milk or water as needed to achieve desired consistency. Season, as desired.

7. **Cashew "Cream" Sauce:** Soak raw cashews (see note) in just enough water to cover, for 1 to 4 hours, then drain and rinse them well. Put the soaked cashews in a blender container and process with a bit of water until smooth, adding more water as needed to achieve desired consistency. Season, as desired.

8. **White Bean "Cream" Sauce:** Drain and rinse 1 can of white beans (any variety). Put the beans in a blender container and process with a bit of unsweetened nondairy milk or water until smooth, adding more nondairy milk or water as needed to achieve desired consistency. Season, as desired.

9. **Walnut "Cream" Sauce:** Put chopped walnuts in a blender container and process with a bit of water until smooth, adding more water as needed to achieve desired consistency. Season, as desired.

10. **Almond "Cream" Sauce:** Put chopped almonds (soak and drain first, if desired) in a blender container and process with a bit of water until smooth, adding more water as needed to achieve desired consistency. Season, as desired.

LAURA'S TOP TEN
TWO-INGREDIENT RECIPES

Sometimes you need a meal or light snack in a hurry, and here are some of my favorite quick fixes when the "hungries" strike and time is at a minimum. Yep, it's true: each of these "recipes" has only two ingredients, but they're all super satisfying and totally tasty!

1. **Tamari-Baked Mushrooms:** Slice portobello or cremini mushrooms, drizzle with tamari and bake in a covered casserole at 375 degrees F for 35 to 45 minutes, or until soft and bubbling.

2. **Kale Marinara:** Wash, remove stems and finely chop kale, then simmer with prepared marinara sauce.

3. **Loaded Sweet Potato:** Bake a sweet potato, slice in half lengthwise and top it with warm canned lentil or black bean soup.

4. **Chili-Topped Baked Potatoes:** Bake a russet potato, slice in half lengthwise and top it with warm canned vegan chili.

5. **Quick Guacamole:** Peel, pit and mash an avocado with some jarred salsa for instant guacamole.

6. **Apples and PB:** Core and slice organic apples, then slather the slices with peanut butter for a quick treat.

7. **Almond Celery Sticks:** Spread celery sticks with almond butter for a healthy snack.

8. **Pink Watermelon Cooler:** Process chilled, cubed watermelon and frozen raspberries in a blender to make a refreshing summer drink.

9. **Banana Smoothie Shake:** Put frozen banana slices and some nondairy milk in a high-performance blending appliance. Process until smooth and creamy to make a quick, refreshing shake.

10. **Avocado-Miso Spread:** Peel and pit one small ripe avocado. Put the avocado in a bowl and add 1 heaping teaspoon of mellow white miso. Vigorously stir to combine. Serve on whole-grain toast or crackers for a quick lunch or pick-me-up snack.

Avocado-Salsa Sandwich (page 153)

LAURA'S TOP TEN
DRIED HERBS AND SPICES

I like to add layers of flavor to my plant-based masterpieces. Incorporating dried herbs and spices into my daily recipes is an easy way to jazz up any meal!

Try to buy herbs and spices that are organic and non-irradiated whenever possible, and store them in a cool, dark place away from sunlight and heat. I keep my dried herbs and spices organized (in alphabetical order), and stored in an easily accessible drawer in my kitchen. Check the expiration dates on your herbs and spices every six months and replace items that are past their prime.

Adding dried herbs and spices to your daily cooking allows you to put your individual stamp on a variety of dishes, creating appetizing meals that your family will appreciate, without adding a lot of extra salt, sugar or fat to your recipes.

In addition to salt and pepper, here is my top ten list of *herbs and spices* that I keep regularly stocked in my kitchen spice drawer.

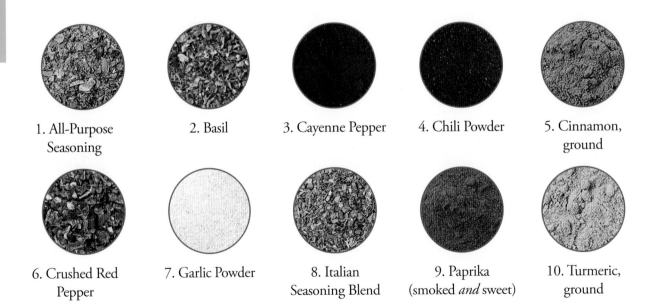

1. All-Purpose Seasoning
2. Basil
3. Cayenne Pepper
4. Chili Powder
5. Cinnamon, ground
6. Crushed Red Pepper
7. Garlic Powder
8. Italian Seasoning Blend
9. Paprika (smoked *and* sweet)
10. Turmeric, ground

A WORD ABOUT SALT AND PEPPER

I like using Himalayan pink salt or sea salt in my recipes. My choice for black pepper is the freshly ground variety.

Why aren't *exact* amounts of salt and pepper always included in some of the recipes in this book? If a recipe requires a precise amount of salt or pepper to make it taste optimal, the exact amount is included in the ingredients list. If the inclusion of either salt or pepper is only a matter of choice, I have left it up to you to season as desired.

Jazz singer Kelle Jolly and Laura prepare *Root Veggie and Lentil Trio Stew* (page 204).

TABLE OF EQUIVALENT MEASURES

No matter how many times I measure ingredients in my recipes, I never seem to remember the table of equivalent measures. This table is convenient to refer to when doubling or tripling recipes, cooking up new recipes or cutting an existing recipe in half. I know you'll find it as handy as I do!

This...	Equals This...
3 teaspoons	1 tablespoon
4 tablespoons	¼ cup
5 tablespoons plus 1 teaspoon	⅓ cup
8 tablespoons	½ cup
12 tablespoons	¾ cup
16 tablespoons	1 cup (or 8 ounces)
2 cups	1 pint (or 16 ounces)
4 cups	1 quart (or 32 ounces)
4 quarts	1 gallon (or 128 ounces)

CHAPTER TWO
Festive Morning Favorites

A breakfast scramble, fun frittata, power oatmeal, vegan "French" toast or mini-quiches are all fabulous ways to start the day. When the morning starts with a festive meal, good things are sure to follow!

Recipes

18

Baked Potato Tofu Scramble

MAKES 4 TO 6 SERVINGS

Here tofu and potatoes are served as a tasty breakfast scramble, making great use of leftover baked potatoes. I try to bake a few extra spuds whenever I bake potatoes, so I have cooked potatoes to use in a scramble, for baked home fries, vegan frittatas, twice-baked potatoes and so much more!

- 1 large sweet onion, sliced

- 3 tablespoons water, plus more as needed

- 3 teaspoons extra-virgin olive oil, divided

- 2 teaspoons Italian seasoning blend, divided

- 2 teaspoons tamari, divided

- 8 ounces white button mushrooms, sliced

- 2 large baked potatoes, with peels on, chilled and cubed

- 3 to 4 medium kale leaves, stems removed and thinly sliced

- 1 block (14 to 16 ounces) extra-firm regular tofu, drained

- 1 teaspoon ground turmeric

- ½ teaspoon smoked paprika

- ⅛ teaspoon cayenne pepper

- ¾ cup shredded vegan cheese

- Sea salt, to taste

- Freshly ground black pepper, to taste

Put the onion, 3 tablespoons water, 1 teaspoon olive oil, 1 teaspoon Italian seasoning blend and 1 teaspoon tamari in a large nonstick skillet. Cover and cook over medium-low heat for 5 to 6 minutes, stirring occasionally. Add the mushrooms, cover and cook, stirring occasionally, for 5 to 6 minutes, adding more water, as needed, if the pan becomes dry.

Add the cubed baked potatoes, 1 teaspoon olive oil and 2 tablespoons water, cover and cook, stirring occasionally, for about 10 minutes, or until the potatoes begin to brown. Add the kale and a bit more water if the pan is dry, cover and cook for 3 minutes, stirring occasionally.

While the potato mixture cooks, put the tofu, turmeric, smoked paprika, cayenne pepper, 1 teaspoon Italian seasoning blend, 1 teaspoon olive oil and 1 teaspoon tamari into a medium-sized bowl and mash with a potato masher or large fork, until it becomes the consistency of cooked scrambled eggs.

Add the tofu mixture to the potato mixture, and add a bit more water if the pan is dry. Cover and cook for 5 minutes. Sprinkle with the vegan cheese and cook for 5 minutes more, stirring occasionally, until the cheese is melted and the scramble has become slightly golden around the edges.

Taste, and add sea salt and freshly ground pepper, if desired. Serve garnished with sliced avocado, with toast on the side, if desired.

Portobello-Broccoli Tofu Scramble

MAKES 3 TO 4 SERVINGS

Meaty tasting portobello mushrooms, combined with fresh broccoli, present a hearty and substantial "top-o-the-morning" scramble. This effective egg substitute does double duty served as the star of a festive brunch or light supper entrée.

- 2 large portobello mushrooms, stems removed, gills removed (see note) and diced

- 1 small sweet onion, diced

- 3 tablespoons water, plus more as needed

- 2½ teaspoons extra-virgin olive oil, divided

- 3 teaspoons reduced-sodium tamari, divided

- 1½ teaspoons Italian seasoning blend, divided

- 2 cups bite-sized broccoli florets

- 1 block (14 to 16 ounces) extra-firm regular tofu, drained

- 1 teaspoon ground turmeric

- ⅛ teaspoon cayenne pepper

- ½ cup shredded vegan cheese (optional)

Put the mushrooms, onion, water, 2 teaspoons olive oil, 2 teaspoons tamari and 1 teaspoon Italian seasoning blend into a large non-stick skillet. Cover and cook over medium heat, stirring occasionally, for 5 to 7 minutes, or until the mushrooms begin to soften. Decrease the heat to medium-low and add the broccoli, cover and cook, stirring occasionally, for 3 minutes.

Meanwhile, put the tofu, ½ teaspoon olive oil, ½ teaspoon Italian seasoning blend, turmeric and cayenne pepper into a medium-sized bowl, and mash, using a potato masher or large fork, until crumbly. Add the tofu mixture to the mushroom-broccoli mixture in the skillet. Cover and cook, stirring occasionally, for about 5 minutes, or until the tofu is heated through. Add the optional vegan cheese and cook for 2 to 3 minutes, or until the vegan cheese has melted and the scramble is slightly golden around the edges. Remove the pan from the heat, cover and let stand 3 to 5 minutes for the scramble to "set." Serve with *Cinnamon-Sugar Crisps* (page 59) on the side.

CHEF'S NOTE: To remove the gills from a portobello mushroom, use a spoon (a grapefruit spoon works well) to carefully scoop out the dark areas (the gills) from the underside of the mushroom.

21

Classic Morning Scramble

MAKES 3 TO 4 SERVINGS

Onions, mushrooms and peppers combined with soft tofu make this vegan scramble a tasty twist on an American classic. Spiced up with a generous amount of Dijon mustard, some turmeric and a bit of Italian seasoning, this satisfying combination will truly be a hit at your morning table.

- 1 large red onion, peeled and chopped
- 1 tablespoon extra-virgin olive oil
- 1 teaspoon Italian seasoning blend
- 2 teaspoons tamari, divided
- ½ teaspoon smoked paprika
- 1 tablespoon water, plus more as needed
- 8 ounces cremini mushrooms, sliced
- 1½ medium yellow sweet bell peppers, cored, seeded and chopped
- 16 to 20 ounces soft regular tofu, well drained
- 2 tablespoons Dijon mustard (see note)
- ½ teaspoon ground turmeric
- ½ cup vegan cheese

Put the onion, olive oil, Italian seasoning, 1 teaspoon tamari and smoked paprika in a large non-stick skillet. Add 1 tablespoon of water, cover and cook over medium heat, stirring occasionally, for 5 minutes, or until the onion becomes translucent. Add the mushrooms and a bit more water, if the pan is dry. Cover and cook for 5 to 7 minutes, stirring occasionally. Add the bell pepper. Cover and cook for 3 to 4 minutes, stirring occasionally, until the pepper begins to soften.

Meanwhile, put the tofu, mustard, 1 teaspoon tamari and turmeric in a medium-sized bowl and mash using a potato masher or large fork, until it resembles the consistency of scrambled eggs. Add the mashed tofu to the skillet, cover and cook for 3 minutes, stirring occasionally, or until the tofu begins to brown. Decrease the heat to medium-low, add the vegan cheese, cover and cook for 6 to 10 minutes, stirring occasionally, or until the scramble is slightly golden and the tofu is cooked through. Serve with *"Lemony Maple-Cranberry Muffins"* (page 88) and fresh fruit on the side, if desired.

CHEF'S NOTE: For a more subtle "mustardy" taste, decrease the amount of Dijon mustard to 1 tablespoon, or you may omit the Dijon mustard entirely, if preferred.

Potato and Spinach "Frittata"

MAKES 3 TO 4 SERVINGS

It's frittata time! This authentic-tasting frittata is baked in the oven, making it especially easy to prepare. With a delicious potato/onion base, paired with an herb-infused egg-like filling, this egg-less entrée is a true winner, perfect to serve for any meal of the day.

POTATO LAYER

- ¼ cup water, plus more as needed
- 1 teaspoon reduced-sodium tamari
- 2 large red or white potatoes (with peel on) very thinly sliced
- 1 teaspoon Italian seasoning blend
- ½ cup minced sweet onion

"EGG" LAYER

- 2 tablespoons rolled oats
- 1 block (14 to 16 ounces), extra-firm regular tofu, drained
- 3 tablespoons nondairy milk
- 1 teaspoon Italian seasoning blend
- ½ teaspoon reduced-sodium tamari
- ¼ teaspoon ground turmeric

ADDITIONAL INGREDIENTS

- ¼ teaspoon sea salt
- 4 cups baby spinach
- ⅛ teaspoon smoked paprika

Preheat the oven to 375 degrees F. Liberally coat a 9 to 10-inch round quiche dish with vegan margarine.

Put the "potato layer" ingredients in a large skillet in the order listed. Cover and cook on medium-low heat for 15 to 18 minutes, or until the potatoes are almost fork tender, flipping them over half way though cooking. Check often and add more water, 2 tablespoons at a time, as needed to prevent sticking.

Meanwhile, put the rolled oats in a blender and process into coarse flour. Add the tofu, nondairy milk, Italian seasoning, tamari and turmeric and process until smooth.

Arrange all of the potatoes in an overlapping, even layer in the prepared dish. Sprinkle ¼ teaspoon sea salt over the top. Spread one-third of the tofu mixture evenly over the potatoes. Top with the spinach, pressing it down firmly. Carefully pour the remaining tofu mixture over the spinach and gently spread it in an even layer, using a rubber spatula.

Sprinkle the paprika over the top of the frittata. Tent with foil and bake for 30 minutes. Remove the foil and bake for 15 to 20 minutes more, or until the frittata is set. Put the dish on a wire rack and loosen the sides of the frittata with a knife. Let cool 12 to 15 minutes and slice into wedges. Serve warm.

Mini-Quiche Cups

MAKES 6 SERVINGS

These tasty little quiche-bites are easy to whip up for an early morning meal or impressive brunch treat. Tofu stands in for the eggs and cream, while vegan cheese pairs with fresh broccoli to make a satisfying dish.

- 1 block (14 to 16 ounces) extra-firm regular tofu, well drained and broken into pieces
- ½ tablespoon extra-virgin olive oil
- ½ tablespoon reduced-sodium or regular tamari
- 1 teaspoon Dijon mustard
- ¼ teaspoon smoked paprika
- ¼ teaspoon garlic powder
- ½ cup shredded vegan cheddar-style cheese
- 2 cups diced broccoli florets (reserve 6 small florets for garnish)
- 6 grape tomatoes, sliced in half

Preheat the oven to 375 degrees F. Generously coat a 6-cup jumbo muffin pan with vegan margarine.

Put the tofu, olive oil, tamari, Dijon mustard, paprika and garlic powder in a high-performance blending appliance and process until smooth. Stir in the shredded cheese and broccoli, using a small rubber spatula. Divide the tofu mixture into the prepared muffin cups, and smooth the tops. Decorate each quiche with 2 tomato halves and 1 broccoli floret. Loosely cover the quiches with a large piece of parchment paper.

Bake for 15 minutes. Take the pan out of the oven and remove the parchment paper. Bake uncovered for an additional 10 to 12 minutes, or until the mini-quiches are almost set. Put the pan on a wire rack and loosen the sides of each quiche with a knife.

Let cool for 5 to 7 minutes. Place a large piece of parchment paper on a cutting board or large sheet pan, and carefully invert the muffin pan, releasing the quiches from the muffin cups. Gently and carefully turn the quiches upright onto the wire rack, and let cool an additional 5 minutes before serving.

Rice 'n Date Breakfast Bowl

MAKES 3 TO 4 SERVINGS

This hearty bowl makes for substantial breakfast fare. Baked in the oven, it's a great choice for busy mornings. This recipe is easily doubled or tripled to feed a crowd!

- 1 cup long grain brown rice, uncooked
- ½ cup unsweetened shredded dried coconut
- ½ teaspoon ground cinnamon
- ½ teaspoon vanilla extract
- 6 large Medjool dates, pitted and chopped
- 3 cups water
- 2 tablespoons maple syrup, plus more as needed
- Nondairy milk, for serving

Preheat the oven to 375 degrees F. Put the rice, coconut, cinnamon, vanilla and dates into a medium-sized casserole dish with a tight fitting lid. Stir to combine. Pour the water over the rice mixture and gently stir to combine.

Cover and bake for 40 to 45 minutes, or until the water is almost absorbed and the rice is soft. Remove from the oven, uncover and drizzle the maple syrup over the top. Cover and bake for 5 to 10 minutes more. Put the dish on a wire rack and let stand for 20 minutes before serving. Serve with nondairy milk and more maple syrup on the side, if desired.

Breakfast Tostadas

MAKES 4 SERVINGS

Tostadas are a flavor-packed and colorful way to start the day. Packed with nutrient-dense veggies and spices, this spicy option will start your morning off with a smile.

- 1 large sweet onion, chopped

- 3 teaspoons extra-virgin olive oil, divided

- 2 teaspoons chili powder, divided

- ⅛ teaspoon cayenne pepper

- 1 large portobello mushroom, gills removed (see note on page 20) and chopped

- 2 teaspoons tamari, divided

- 1 tablespoon water, plus more as needed

- 1 medium green pepper, seeded and chopped

- 1 small zucchini, chopped

- 1 block (14 to 16 ounces) firm or extra-firm regular tofu, drained

- ½ teaspoon ground turmeric

- 3 tablespoons shredded vegan cheese

- 4 large whole-grain tortillas (each about 10-inches in diameter)

- 4 heaping tablespoons prepared salsa, plus more for serving

- 2 small avocados, peeled, pitted and sliced

Preheat the oven to 375 degrees F. Line a large, rimmed baking sheet with unbleached parchment paper.

Put the onion, 2 teaspoons olive oil, 1 teaspoon chili powder and cayenne pepper into a large sauté pan. Cover and cook, stirring frequently, over medium heat for 5 to 6 minutes. Add the mushrooms, 1 teaspoon tamari and 1 tablespoon water. Cover and cook, stirring occasionally, for 5 minutes, adding more water, 2 tablespoons at a time, if the pan becomes dry.

Add the green pepper and zucchini, cover and cook, stirring frequently, for 5 minutes, adding more water, 1 tablespoon at a time, if the pan becomes dry.

While the vegetables cook, put the tofu, 1 teaspoon tamari, 1 teaspoon oil, ½ teaspoon turmeric and 1 teaspoon chili powder into a medium-sized bowl, and mash using a potato masher or large fork until the mixture resembles scrambled eggs. Decrease the heat to medium-low. Add the tofu mixture to the vegetable mixture. Cover and cook for 5 minutes, stirring frequently.

Add the vegan cheese, cover and cook for 5 minutes, stirring occasionally, until the tofu is slightly golden around the edges.

Meanwhile, arrange the tortillas in a single layer on the prepared baking sheet. Bake for 5 to 8 minutes, checking frequently, until the tortillas are crisp around the edges.

For each serving, put 1 tortilla in the center of a plate. Spoon one-quarter of the tofu mixture onto the center of the tortilla. Top with 1 heaping tablespoon salsa and garnish with several avocado slices. Serve hot with more salsa on the side, if desired.

Mostly Millet Breakfast Pudding

MAKES 4 SERVINGS

This refreshing change to hot porridge highlights millet as the star ingredient. Cooking in about 25 minutes, this combo makes a hearty breakfast option. Millet is gluten free, making it a wonderful choice when serving breakfast to family members or overnight guests with wheat sensitivities. The creamy and delicious texture, paired with a hint of coconut and cinnamon, makes this pudding a perfect alternative to oatmeal any morning of the week!

- 2½ cups water, plus more as needed
- 1 cup millet, rinsed
- ⅓ cup raisins
- 2 tablespoons unsweetened shredded dried coconut
- ½ teaspoon ground cinnamon
- ⅛ teaspoon sea salt
- Maple syrup, for serving (optional)
- Nondairy milk, for serving (optional)

Put the water, millet, raisins, coconut, cinnamon and salt into a large saucepan. Bring to a boil over medium heat. Decrease the heat to low, cover and cook for about 25 minutes, stirring occasionally, until most of the liquid has been absorbed and the mixture is creamy. Remove from heat. Cover and let stand for about 5 minutes. Serve with maple syrup and nondairy milk on the side, if desired.

CHEF'S NOTE: After the millet pudding is cooked, it will stay warm for about 20 minutes in the covered saucepan, which is ideal for family members who trickle in for breakfast.

Oatmeal, Polenta and Berry Breakfast Casserole

MAKES 2 TO 3 SERVINGS

CASSEROLE

- ⅔ cup rolled oats
- ¼ cup unsweetened shredded dried coconut
- 3 tablespoons polenta (corn grits)
- ½ teaspoon ground cinnamon
- ½ teaspoon vanilla extract
- ⅛ teaspoon sea salt

- 2 tablespoons sweetened dried cranberries
- 2 tablespoons raisins
- 1½ cups water
- 1 cup nondairy milk (vanilla flavored is nice), plus more for serving
- 1 tablespoon maple syrup

TOPPING

- 2 tablespoons dark brown sugar or maple syrup, plus more to taste

This simple casserole cooks in the oven while you go about your morning rituals, offering a satisfying dish to keep you sustained well into the afternoon.

Preheat the oven to 375 degrees F. Put all of the casserole ingredients into a medium-sized baking dish and stir to combine. Cover and bake for 30 to 40 minutes, or until almost all of the liquid is absorbed and the casserole is bubbling. Remove from oven, uncover and sprinkle with brown sugar or maple syrup to taste. Cover and let stand 5 to 7 minutes. Serve with more nondairy milk on the side, if desired.

Crunchy-Nutty Oatmeal and Raisin Granola

MAKES ABOUT 5 CUPS

This granola is easy to make and easier to eat, making a welcome breakfast cereal or yummy afternoon snack.

- 2½ cups rolled oats
- ½ cup raw almonds
- ½ cup raw cashews
- ⅓ cup raw or roasted sunflower seeds
- ¼ cup sesame seeds
- ¼ cup toasted wheat germ
- ½ cup maple syrup
- ¼ cup vegetable oil (I like the fruity flavor of extra-virgin olive oil)
- 1 teaspoon vanilla extract
- ¾ cup raisins

Preheat the oven to 350 degrees F. Line an 11 by 17-inch rimmed baking sheet with unbleached parchment paper.

Put the oats, almonds, cashews, sunflower seeds, sesame seeds and wheat germ into a large bowl and stir to combine. Put the maple syrup, vegetable oil and vanilla into a small bowl and stir to combine.

Pour the maple syrup mixture over the oat/nut mixture. Stir to thoroughly coat.

Spread the mixture in an even layer on the prepared baking sheet. Bake for 18 to 20 minutes, or until almost golden brown, checking often, and stirring every 7 to 10 minutes. Remove the baking sheet from the oven and stir in the raisins. Bake for 3 to 5 minutes more, or until the granola is golden. Transfer to a large bowl. Set the bowl on a wire rack, and let cool for 30 minutes, stirring occasionally, so the granola does not stick together. Store in the refrigerator, tightly covered, for up to 3 days.

Fabulous French Toast Bake

MAKES 4 TO 6 SERVINGS

My mother-in-law has a wonderful recipe for baked French toast. I decided to veganize it so I could make it for my family and friends (and myself!). I adore the classic taste of this delightful breakfast treat.

- ¾ block (10 to 12 ounces) firm or extra-firm regular tofu, drained
- 1 medium ripe banana
- ½ tablespoon extra-virgin olive oil
- 1 teaspoon vanilla extract
- 1 teaspoon ground cinnamon, divided
- 1 cup nondairy milk
- 8 to 12 slices country-style or Tuscan-style bread
- 4 tablespoons dark brown sugar
- 3 tablespoons vegan margarine
- Maple syrup or fruit preserves, for serving

Liberally coat an 11 by 17-inch rimmed baking pan with vegan margarine.

Put the tofu, banana, olive oil, vanilla, ½ teaspoon cinnamon and nondairy milk into a blender and process until smooth.

Arrange the bread slices in a single layer on the prepared pan. Poke multiple holes in each slice with a dinner fork (this will allow the banana/tofu mixture to be more readily absorbed into the bread). Pour the banana/tofu mixture over the bread and gently push the mixture into the bread slices, using a spatula. Refrigerate for at least 1 hour for the banana/tofu mixture to permeate the bread (see note).

Preheat the oven to 375 degrees F. Remove the bread from the refrigerator. Dust the bread slices with about ½ teaspoon of cinnamon. Tent with foil and bake for 20 minutes (see note), or until the top of the bread is starting to become golden.

While the toast cooks, put the vegan margarine and brown sugar in a small bowl and mix together with a fork until well combined.

Remove the toast from the oven and put it on a wire rack. Remove the foil and cut the slices apart (they will have baked together at this point). Dot the top of each piece of toast with the vegan margarine/brown sugar mixture. Bake uncovered for 10 to 20 minutes more, checking often, or until browned and crisp on both sides. If the bottom of the toast is getting *too* brown, flip each slice over during the last 5 to 15 minutes of baking (see note). Serve topped with maple syrup or your favorite fruit preserves, if desired.

CHEF'S NOTES:

- You may prepare the casserole the night before, tent with foil and refrigerate overnight. Proceed with baking as directed.
- The length of baking time will vary, depending on the thickness of your bread.

Preparing *Fabulous French Toast Bake* (page 34)

Maple, Walnut and Oat Breakfast Bites

MAKES 12 "BITES"

These not-too-sweet treats are a lovely way to start your day. Made with wholesome ingredients, theses gems are great for an on-the-go breakfast, mid-morning coffee break or after school snack!

- 2 large bananas
- 5 tablespoons maple syrup, divided
- 1 teaspoon vanilla extract
- 1½ cups rolled oats
- ⅓ cup sweetened dried cranberries
- ½ cup chopped walnuts
- 3 tablespoons freshly ground flaxseeds

Preheat the oven to 375 degrees F. Line a 12-cup standard muffin tin with paper liners.

Put the bananas, 3 tablespoons maple syrup and vanilla into a medium-sized bowl and mash into a chunky purée using a potato masher or large fork. Add the oats, cranberries, walnuts and freshly ground flaxseeds and stir to combine. Divide among the prepared muffin cups and smooth the tops.

Bake for 20 to 24 minutes, or until set in the center and slightly golden around the edges. Put the tin on a wire rack and let cool 5 minutes.

Put the remaining 2 tablespoons maple syrup into a small bowl. Spread maple syrup liberally over the top of each "bite" using a pastry brush or back of a small spoon. Transfer the "bites" to a wire rack and let cool 10 to 15 minutes before serving. Stored in a tightly covered container in the refrigerator, leftovers will keep about 2 days.

CHAPTER THREE
Sunny Smoothies

Nothin' starts off the day in a more refreshing way than a frosty smoothie. From fruit smoothies to smoothie bowls, green smoothies or tropical-style smoothies, these delightful drinks are both nutritious *and* delicious!

Recipes

39

Banana-Berry Smoothie

MAKES 1 TO 2 SERVINGS

Yummy! This refreshing smoothie combines the sweet taste of ripe bananas with frozen berries to make a satisfying good-morning sip.

- 2 tablespoons flaxseeds
- ⅓ cup nondairy milk, plus more as needed
- 1 large frozen banana
- 1 medium navel orange, peeled, seeded and chopped
- ½ cup frozen mixed berries
- 2 Medjool dates, pitted and chopped

Put the flaxseeds into a high-performance blending appliance and process into fine flour. Add the remaining ingredients and process until smooth and creamy, adding more nondairy milk, as needed, to achieve the desired consistency. Serve immediately.

Berry-Date Delight Smoothie

MAKES 1 SERVING

This luscious mixed-berry and sweet date smoothie is truly delightful. It is so thick and creamy, you can eat it with a spoon!

- **2 tablespoons flaxseeds**
- **1 cup baby spring greens mix**
- **1 cup frozen mixed berries (strawberries, blueberries, raspberries, etc.)**
- **2 large Medjool dates, pitted and chopped**
- **½ cup nondairy milk, plus more as needed**

Put the flaxseeds into a high-performance blending appliance and process into fine flour.

Add the greens, berries, dates and ½ cup nondairy milk. Blend until smooth, adding more nondairy milk, as needed, to achieve the desired consistency. Serve immediately.

Blueberry and Cantaloupe Pie Smoothie Bowl

MAKES 1 SERVING

This scrumptious smoothie tastes super refreshing. Sweet cantaloupe is blended with bananas and topped with crunchy almonds and plump, fresh blueberries, making a welcome wake up meal in a bowl!

- 1½ cups peeled, seeded and cubed cantaloupe
- 1 very large frozen banana
- ⅛ teaspoon ground cinnamon
- 8 to 10 raw almonds
- 14 to 16 blueberries

Put the cantaloupe, banana and cinnamon into a high-performance blending appliance and process until smooth and creamy. Pour into a serving bowl and garnish with the raw almonds and fresh blueberries. Serve immediately.

Pineapple and Coconut Green Delight

MAKES 1 TO 2 SERVINGS

This luscious smoothie reminds me of being in the tropics with the welcoming combo of coconut, sweet dates, juicy pineapple and a frozen banana, making it extra frosty and thick.

- 2 tablespoons flaxseeds
- 1 cup loosely packed chopped romaine lettuce
- 1 cup peeled and cubed pineapple
- 1 large frozen banana
- 2 large Medjool dates, pitted and chopped
- 1 tablespoon unsweetened shredded dried coconut
- 1 cup nondairy milk

Put the flaxseeds into a high-performance blending appliance and process into fine flour.

Add the remaining ingredients and process until smooth and creamy. Serve immediately.

46

Green Julius Smoothie

MAKES 1 TO 2 SERVINGS

Reminiscent of a classic New York City drink, this refreshing smoothie makes a satisfying breakfast delight.

- 2 tablespoons flaxseeds
- ⅔ cup nondairy milk, plus more as needed
- 1 large navel orange, peeled, seeded and chopped
- 1 large frozen banana
- 1 cup baby spinach
- 2 large Medjool dates, pitted and chopped

Put the flaxseeds into a high-performance blending appliance and process into fine flour. Add the remaining ingredients and process until smooth and creamy, adding more nondairy milk, as needed, to achieve the desired consistency. Serve immediately.

Purple Machine Smoothie

MAKES 1 TO 2 SERVINGS

The pretty color of this luscious, nutrient dense smoothie adds pizzazz to your morning.

- 2 tablespoons flaxseeds
- 1 cup chopped romaine lettuce
- 1 cup frozen mixed berries (strawberries, blueberries, raspberries, etc.)
- 1 large frozen banana
- 1 large stalk of celery
- ½ cup water, plus more as needed

Put the flaxseeds into a high-performance blender and process into fine flour.

Add the remaining ingredients and process until smooth and creamy, adding more water, as needed, to achieve the desired consistency. Serve immediately.

Kale-icious Smoothie Bowl with Orange Cream Swirl

MAKES 2 SERVINGS

This delightful smoothie bowl features nutritious kale and sweet dark berries, topped with a pretty orange swirl. This tasty combination makes a colorful, refreshing and healthy breakfast treat.

- 2 tablespoons flaxseeds

- 1 large navel orange, peeled, seeded and chopped

- ¼ block (3 to 4 ounces) firm regular tofu, drained

- 1 cup firmly packed kale, remove stems before chopping

- 1½ large frozen bananas

- 1 cup frozen berries, plus more as desired

- ⅓ cup nondairy milk

- 2 teaspoons raw or roasted sunflower seeds

Put the flaxseeds into a high-performance blending appliance and process into fine flour. Transfer the flaxseeds to a small bowl.

Put the chopped orange and tofu into a high-performance blending appliance, and process until smooth. Transfer the orange/tofu mixture into a small bowl, leaving about ½ cup of the orange/tofu mixture in the blender container.

Add the ground flaxseeds to the orange/tofu mixture in the blender container. Add the kale, banana, berries and nondairy milk to the blender. Process until smooth and creamy, adding more frozen berries if the mixture seems too thin (mixture should be quite thick, but smooth and creamy at the same time).

Pour the berry/banana/kale mixture into 2 medium-sized serving bowls. Drizzle the orange/tofu mixture (that was reserved in the small bowl) over the top and swirl it in with a spoon. Garnish each bowl with the sunflower seeds and a few additional berries. Serve immediately.

Banana-Mango Smoothie

MAKES 1 TO 2 SERVINGS

This lively drink combines a fresh, ripe banana with frozen mangos to make a colorful, thick, creamy and delicious smoothie.

- 1 tablespoon nondairy milk, plus more as needed

- 1 large, very ripe banana

- 2 cups peeled and pitted frozen mango slices

- 2 tablespoons maple syrup, plus more as needed

Put all of the ingredients into a high-performance blending appliance and process until smooth and creamy, adding more nondairy milk and/or maple syrup, as needed, to achieve the desired taste and consistency. Serve immediately.

50

CHAPTER FOUR

Nibbles, Noshes and Quick Bites

Woo-hoo! I am a big fan of *snacks!* Getting away from crackers, chips and cookies can be challenging, but sometimes a piece of fresh fruit just won't do. So here I am sharing several of my favorite nibbles to serve, whether you are hosting a big party or having an afternoon bite.

Recipes

53

Miso-Parsley Hummus

MAKES 4 SERVINGS

Miso provides texture and taste to this hummus without adding any oil, keeping it a light and low-fat option for a satisfying snack.

- 1 can (15 to 16 ounces) chickpeas (garbanzo beans), drained and rinsed

- 2 to 3 tablespoons water, plus more as needed

- 2 tablespoons freshly squeezed lemon juice (see note)

- 1 tablespoon chopped fresh parsley

- 1 tablespoon mellow white miso

- ¼ teaspoon cayenne pepper

- ¼ teaspoon sea salt

Put all of the ingredients into a blender and process until smooth. Add a bit more water, as needed, to achieve the desired consistency.

CHEF'S NOTE: For an extra "lemony" taste, use 3 tablespoons lemon juice.

Chunky Guacamole

- 2 large ripe avocados
- 2 tablespoons freshly squeezed lemon juice
- 1 teaspoon chili powder
- ¼ teaspoon ground turmeric
- ¼ teaspoon smoked paprika
- ¼ teaspoon sea salt, plus more as needed
- ¹⁄₁₆ to ⅛ teaspoon cayenne pepper
- 1 medium tomato, diced
- ½ medium sweet onion, diced

This yummy guacamole features zesty spices and ripe avocados, combined with diced tomatoes and onions to add texture and taste.

Peel, pit and rough chop the avocados. Put the avocados, lemon juice, chili powder, turmeric, smoked paprika, sea salt and cayenne pepper in a medium-sized bowl and mash with a potato masher or large fork until combined. Gently fold in the tomatoes and onion. Serve immediately.

56

Smoky and Spicy Guacamole

MAKES 4 TO 6 SERVINGS

This dandy dip has a real zing to it, incorporating a pleasing combination of ripe avocados enhanced by fresh lemon juice and piquant spices.

- 2 large ripe avocados
- 2 tablespoons freshly squeezed lemon juice
- 1 small clove garlic, minced
- 1 teaspoon chili powder
- ½ teaspoon smoked paprika
- ¼ teaspoon sea salt, plus more as needed
- ⅛ teaspoon cayenne pepper

Peel, pit and rough chop the avocados. Put the chopped avocados, lemon juice, garlic, chili powder, smoked paprika, sea salt and cayenne pepper into a medium-sized bowl and mash with a potato masher or large fork until combined. Serve immediately or cover and refrigerate up to 1 hour before serving.

Guacamole Mini-Peppers

MAKES 6 SERVINGS

These simple nibbles were such a hit at my New Year's Day party last year, I just *had* to share! Using pre-made guacamole makes this recipe super quick, but for a more customized version, use my recipe for *Smoky and Spicy Guacamole* (page 56).

- 12 to 16 ounces guacamole

- 1 package (8 ounces) sweet mini peppers, cut in half lengthwise and seeded

- ½ teaspoon chili powder, plus more as needed

Put a heaping tablespoon of the guacamole into each pepper half. Arrange the peppers in a pleasing manner on a pretty platter. Dust with chili powder, to taste. Serve immediately or cover and refrigerate for up to 1 hour before serving.

Polenta Pizza Bites

MAKES 4 TO 6 SERVINGS

A gluten-free appetizer is useful to have on hand when entertaining a crowd. These petite bites make a fun, light lunch too and are particularly kid-friendly. This recipe is easily doubled or tripled, and the polenta can be prepared up to 2 days prior to assembling, making this an ideal appetizer for a big party!

POLENTA CRUST

- 1½ cups water, plus more as needed
- ½ cup polenta (corn grits)
- ½ teaspoon dried basil
- ¼ teaspoon sea salt

TOPPING

- 9 heaping tablespoons vegan marinara sauce
- ½ cup plus 1 tablespoon finely chopped kale, remove stems before chopping (see note)
- 8 queen green olives with pimento, sliced
- 2 heaping tablespoons shredded vegan cheese (optional)

Make the polenta by bringing the water to a boil in a medium-sized saucepan over medium heat. Decrease the heat to medium-low. Pour the polenta steadily into the water while stirring constantly. Stir in the basil and salt. Decrease the heat to low.

Cook for 25 to 30 minutes, stirring frequently, until thickened. (The polenta is ready when it easily comes away from the side of the pan and supports a wooden spoon.) Pour the polenta into an 8-inch square baking pan and gently spread it into an even layer using a rubber spatula. Refrigerate for 1 to 2 hours, or until firm to the touch (see note). Cut the cold polenta into 9 squares.

Preheat the oven to 400 degrees F. Line a medium-sized, rimmed baking pan with unbleached parchment paper. Spread 1 heaping tablespoon of the marinara sauce onto a polenta square. Arrange 1 tablespoon of the kale over the sauce. Arrange one-ninth of the olive slices over the kale. Put the polenta square onto the prepared baking sheet. Repeat with the remaining polenta squares.

Bake for 25 minutes. Remove from the oven and top with the optional vegan cheese, if using. Bake for an additional 5 to 10 minutes or until kale is wilted and vegan cheese is melted. Serve warm.

VARIATION: Polenta-Artichoke Pizza Bites — Substitute 8 marinated artichoke hearts, thinly sliced, for the queen olives. Proceed with recipe as directed.

CHEF'S NOTES:
- If desired, you may use finely chopped Swiss chard, broccoli or spinach in place of the kale in this recipe.
- You may prepare the polenta up to 2 days before using it in this recipe.

Cinnamon-Sugar Crisps

MAKES 12 CRISPS

These dainty and versatile crisps are excellent to serve as a sweet side dish to a breakfast scramble, or they pair well with a bowl of soup or crisp green salad for lunch or dinner. They also make a satisfying snack!

• 2 large whole-grain sandwich wraps or tortillas (each about 10-inches in diameter)

• 1 to 2 teaspoons vegan margarine

• 1 heaping tablespoon brown sugar

• ½ teaspoon ground cinnamon

Preheat the oven to 350 degrees F. Line a large, rimmed baking pan with unbleached parchment paper.

Put 1 wrap or tortilla on a dinner plate. Spread a thin layer of vegan margarine over the wrap or tortilla. Repeat with the remaining wrap or tortilla.

Put the brown sugar and cinnamon into a small bowl and stir with a small dry whisk to combine. Divide the cinnamon and sugar mixture evenly onto the wraps or tortillas, spreading in an even layer over the vegan margarine. Cut each wrap or tortilla into six wedges. Arrange the wedges in a single layer on the lined baking pan. Bake for 5 to 6 minutes, checking frequently, until slightly golden and crisp around the edges. Put the pan on a wire rack and cool 10 minutes before serving.

Zesty Maple Almonds

MAKES 10 TO 12 SERVINGS

These sweet and *slightly* spicy almonds are tossed with a flavorsome maple glaze. They can do double duty as an "anytime" snack or snappy appetizer when company is coming.

- 12 ounces raw or roasted almonds
- 2 tablespoons maple syrup
- 2 teaspoons tamari
- 1 teaspoon *Jazzy Sazón* (page 81)

Preheat the oven to 300 degrees F. Line a large baking sheet with unbleached parchment paper. Spread the almonds in an even layer on the prepared baking sheet. Bake for 15 to 20 minutes, checking frequently, or until the almonds are golden brown around the edges.

Carefully transfer the almonds to a large bowl. (*Caution:* the almonds will be very, very hot!) Add the maple syrup, tamari and *Jazzy Sazón* and toss with a large spoon until the almonds are well coated. Transfer the almonds back to the parchment-lined baking sheet and allow them to cool for 30 minutes. Serve warm, or cover tightly and refrigerate. Stored in a tightly covered container in the refrigerator, the almonds will keep for 3 to 4 days.

Nutty Chocolate Chip Trail Mix

MAKES 10 TO 12 SERVINGS

Store-bought trail mix can be quite costly. Making it at home is more cost effective, plus you can customize the mix to suit your tastes. Feel free to swap out the nuts and dried fruit for your favorite varieties to create a favorite "to-go" snack for your family!

- ½ cup raisins
- ½ cup sweetened dried cranberries
- ½ cup vegan chocolate chips
- ½ cup raw or roasted sunflower seeds
- ½ cup chopped pecans
- ½ cup chopped walnuts
- ½ cup raw or roasted almonds

Put all of the ingredients into a medium-sized bowl and gently stir with a large spoon to combine. For an easy "on-the-go" breakfast or snack, divide the trail mix into ten to twelve containers (with tight fitting lids) or ten to twelve individual-sized storage bags and keep on hand for your family members to *grab-n-go*!

Stored in an airtight container in the refrigerator, the trail mix will keep for 2 weeks.

Golden Cashew Milk

MAKES 1 SERVING

- 1 cup sweetened or unsweetened cashew milk

- 1 teaspoon maple syrup, plus more as needed

- ¼ teaspoon ground turmeric

- Dash of freshly ground black pepper

This soothing drink is a great nighttime drink to replace hot tea. Turmeric has a warm, spicy flavor, and when mixed with a bit of sweet maple syrup, it makes a nice nightcap beverage, sans the alcohol. Drink up!

Put all of the ingredients into a small saucepan and whisk to combine. Bring to a simmer over low heat, stirring occasionally. Cook for a few minutes to blend the flavors. Taste and add more maple syrup, if desired. Pour into a mug, let cool slightly and sip.

CHAPTER FIVE

Sauces, Dressings and Tasty Toppings

I believe that adding appetizing essences to vegan recipes is crucial for creating great tasting plant-based food. Whether it's a tasty sauce, zingy dressing, creamy whipped topping or dried herbal-spice blend, these flavor enhancers provide the solid foundation on which delicious vegan recipes are made. Let's jazz it up!

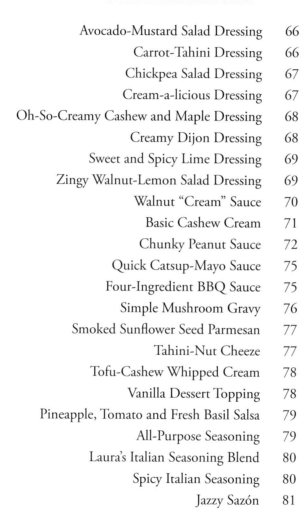

Recipes

Avocado-Mustard Salad Dressing

MAKES ABOUT ¾ CUP

- ½ medium avocado, cut in half, pitted and peeled
- 2 tablespoons freshly squeezed lemon juice
- 2 teaspoons maple syrup
- 1 heaping teaspoon Dijon mustard
- Sea salt, to taste
- Freshly ground black pepper, to taste

This creamy and rich-tasting dressing is wonderful served over a crisp green salad, cooked grains or even potato salad.

Put the avocado, lemon juice, maple syrup and Dijon mustard into a blender and process until smooth. Season with salt and pepper, to taste.

Carrot-Tahini Dressing

MAKES 4 SERVINGS

- ½ cup water, plus more as needed
- 2 small carrots, rough chopped (peeling is optional)
- 2 heaping tablespoons sesame tahini (see note for variation)
- 2 teaspoons freshly squeezed lemon juice
- ½ teaspoon reduced-sodium or regular tamari
- 1 small clove garlic
- Dash cayenne pepper

Fresh carrots and creamy tahini are combined to make a luscious dressing for any type of green salad.

Put all of the ingredients into a blender and process until smooth, adding more water, as needed, to achieve the desired consistency.

VARIATION: Carrot-Miso Dressing—
Use 1 tablespoon of mellow white miso, in place of the tahini, and proceed as directed.

Chickpea Salad Dressing

- ¾ cup cooked chickpeas (garbanzo beans), drained and rinsed, if canned

- ½ cup water, plus more as needed

- 2 teaspoons freshly squeezed lemon juice

- 2 heaping teaspoons sesame tahini

- 1 small clove garlic

- ½ teaspoon reduced-sodium or regular tamari

- ⅛ teaspoon ground turmeric

- ⅛ teaspoon cayenne pepper

- ⅛ teaspoon sea salt, plus more as needed

Easy and nutritious, this dressing is so creamy it will soon become a favorite!

Put all of the ingredients into a blender and process until smooth and creamy. If the dressing is too thick, add a small amount of water, 1 tablespoon at a time, to achieve the desired consistency, pulsing or blending briefly after each addition. Taste and add more sea salt, if desired.

67

Cream-a-licious Dressing

MAKES 4 TO 5 SERVINGS

- 3½ tablespoons vegan mayonnaise

- 1 tablespoon, plus 1 teaspoon Dijon mustard

- 1 tablespoon maple syrup

- ½ teaspoon Italian seasoning blend

- Several grinds of freshly ground black pepper

Oh my gosh! My hubby LOVES this creamy and rich-tasting dressing, and I know you will too. It's so easy to prepare in one minute flat! Drizzle over green salads, steamed veggies, cooked grains or my delightful *Layered Chopped Salad Parfaits* (page 115). Now that's jazzy!

Put the mayonnaise, Dijon mustard, maple syrup, Italian seasoning and freshly ground pepper into a small bowl and whisk briskly until thoroughly combined.

Oh-So-Creamy Cashew and Maple Dressing

- ½ cup chopped raw cashews
- ¼ cup plus 2 tablespoons water
- 2 tablespoons maple syrup
- 1 tablespoon plus 1 teaspoon balsamic vinegar
- 1 tablespoon Dijon mustard
- 1 small clove garlic

My husband says this tastes like the "Honey-Mustard" dressing he used to love. This healthful dressing is delicious on any green salad, and it makes a tasty dipping sauce for veggie sticks too. It can even be drizzled over cooked grains.

Put all of the ingredients into a blender and process until smooth and creamy.

Creamy Dijon Dressing

MAKES 5 TO 6 SERVINGS

This delectable dressing makes a great substitute for egg-and-cream-laden commercial brands. It is so creamy, your diners will not believe that it's vegan!

- 3 heaping tablespoons vegan mayonnaise
- 2 heaping tablespoons Dijon mustard
- 1 tablespoon maple syrup

Put all of the ingredients into a small bowl and briskly whisk until smooth.

68

Sweet and Spicy Lime Dressing

MAKES ABOUT 4 ½ TABLESPOONS

This smooth and flavorful dressing is a breeze to put together, and it adds a pop of zest to any green salad.

- 2½ tablespoons of vegan mayonnaise (see note)
- 1 tablespoon freshly squeezed lime juice
- 1 tablespoon maple syrup
- ¹⁄₁₆ teaspoon of cayenne pepper

Put all of the ingredients into a blender and process until smooth and creamy.

CHEF'S NOTE: For a thicker and creamier dressing, add up to 2 tablespoons more mayonnaise, to taste.

....

Zingy Walnut-Lemon Salad Dressing

MAKES ABOUT 1 ⅔ CUPS

- ¾ cup walnut halves
- ¾ cup water
- 2½ tablespoons freshly squeezed lemon juice
- 1 tablespoon extra-virgin olive oil
- 1 tablespoon Dijon mustard
- 1 tablespoon Italian seasoning blend
- ½ teaspoon maple syrup
- ¼ teaspoon sea salt, to taste
- ¹⁄₁₆ teaspoon cayenne pepper
- Several grinds of freshly ground black pepper, to taste

This smooth and flavorful sauce works equally well served over a crisp green salad, cooked grains or steamed veggies. Hint: No one will miss the dairy cream!

Put all of the ingredients into a blender and process until smooth and creamy. Taste and add more salt and/or pepper, if desired.

Fusilli-Broccoli Bowls with Walnut "Cream" Sauce (page 161)

Walnut "Cream" Sauce

MAKES ABOUT 2 CUPS

- 1½ cups walnut halves
- 1 cup water
- 1 tablespoon maple syrup
- 2 teaspoons tamari
- 2 teaspoons Italian seasoning blend
- 1 medium clove garlic, chopped
- Several grinds of freshly ground black pepper, plus more to taste

When you need a quick and delicious vegan cream sauce to top pasta, salad or veggies, this sauce really shines.

Put all of the ingredients into a blender and process until very smooth and creamy. Taste and add more pepper, if desired. Store tightly covered in the refrigerator for up to 2 days.

Basic Cashew Cream

MAKES ABOUT 1 CUP

This delightful cream substitute is easy to make and can be used in place of dairy cream in many recipes.

- ½ cup raw cashews
- 1¼ cups water, plus more as needed (see note)

Put the cashews into a small bowl and pour about ¾ cup water over the cashews to cover completely. Put the bowl in the refrigerator and let the cashews soak for 1 to 4 hours.

Drain the cashews and rinse with cool running water. Put the soaked cashews into a blender and top with ½ cup water. Blend for about 15 seconds, or until the mixture becomes the consistency of dairy cream. Add more water, if desired, to achieve the desired consistency.

CHEF'S NOTE: For a thicker cashew cream, use less water; for a thinner cashew cream or to achieve a "milk-like" consistency, add more water to achieve the desired consistency.

Chunky Peanut Sauce

MAKES ABOUT ⅓ CUP

With a little bit of spice, a little bit of sweet and a pleasing texture, this enticing dipping sauce pairs well with many dishes. It is also delicious tossed with cooked soba noodles for a quick peanut noodle dish.

- 3 tablespoons water, plus more as needed
- 2 heaping tablespoons chunky peanut butter
- 2 cloves garlic, minced
- ¼ teaspoon sea salt
- ¼ teaspoon chili powder
- ⅛ teaspoon cayenne pepper
- Sea salt, to taste
- Freshly ground black pepper, to taste

Put all of the ingredients into a small bowl and briskly whisk until combined, adding more water, as needed, to achieve the desired consistency. Taste and add sea salt and pepper, if desired.

CHEF'S NOTE: For a sweet sauce, add ½ tablespoon maple syrup. Proceed as directed.

VARIATION: Spicy Peanut Soba Noodles—
Put 4 to 6 ounces of cooked soba or udon noodles into a medium-sized bowl. Pour the *Chunky Peanut Sauce* over the noodles and gently combine, using large tongs. Garnish with sliced scallions and halved grape tomatoes, if desired. Serve warm, or cover, refrigerate and serve cold.

73

Spicy Peanut Soba Noodles

Quick Catsup-Mayo Sauce

MAKES 2 TO 3 SERVINGS

Sunny Black Bean Burgers (page 194)

This simple sauce dresses up vegan burgers, sandwiches or green salads.

- 2 tablespoons vegan mayonnaise, plus more to taste
- 1 heaping tablespoon prepared catsup, plus more to taste

Put the ingredients in a small bowl and briskly whisk to combine. Taste, and add more catsup or mayonnaise, if desired.

VARIATION: Quick Marinara-Mayo Sauce—
Use 1 heaping tablespoon marinara sauce in place of the catsup for a flavorful sauce with an Italian flair.

75

....

Four-Ingredient BBQ Sauce

MAKES ABOUT ⅔ CUP

Do you need a quick BBQ sauce that will impart both sweet *and* spicy flavors to your recipe? This easy to assemble sauce really delivers, making it a delicious option for adding essence and moisture to veggie kebabs, tofu steaks, plant-based burgers or any time you need a tasty barbecue sauce!

- ½ cup catsup
- 2 tablespoons maple syrup
- 1½ teaspoons chili powder
- 1 teaspoon extra-virgin olive oil

Put all of the ingredients into a small bowl and whisk briskly to combine.

Simple Mushroom Gravy

MAKES 6 SERVINGS

I served this gravy to my good friend Shep at a dinner party that I was hosting, and he proclaimed it to be *"the best gravy I've ever had!"* Well, thank you, Shep! (Shhh...I didn't tell him that this is also the *easiest* gravy I've ever made). Bingo.

- 1½ cups plus 3 tablespoons water, divided, plus more as needed
- ¼ large sweet onion, diced
- 12 ounces white button mushrooms, diced
- 1 large vegan bouillon cube, crumbled
- 1½ tablespoons whole wheat flour (see note)

Put 1½ cups water, onion, mushrooms and bouillon cube into a medium-sized saucepan. Cover and bring to a simmer over medium-high heat. Decrease the heat to medium-low and cook for 20 to 25 minutes, stirring occasionally.

Meanwhile, put the flour and 3 tablespoons water into a jar with a tight fitting lid and shake vigorously until smooth. Pour the flour/water mixture into the simmering mushroom gravy in a steady stream, briskly whisking as you go, so the flour mixture does not become lumpy.

Cook, stirring frequently, until the gravy begins to thicken. Decrease the heat to low, cover and simmer, stirring occasionally, for 20 to 30 minutes more, or until the gravy has cooked down and reaches the desired consistency. Serve hot.

CHEF'S NOTE: This gravy has a delicate, thin consistency. For a thicker gravy, use an additional 1 tablespoon of the whole wheat flour. Proceed with recipe as directed.

Smoked Sunflower Seed Parmesan

MAKES 8 SERVINGS

This tasty cheese substitute whips up in no time and tastes great sprinkled over your favorite pasta, chili, cooked casseroles or green salad.

- ½ cup roasted, salted sunflower seeds

- ⅛ teaspoon smoked paprika

Put the sunflower seeds and paprika into a blender and process until they are the consistency of grated Parmesan cheese. Store tightly covered in refrigerator for up to 5 days.

Tahini-Nut Cheeze

MAKES ABOUT 2 CUPS

This dazzling *cheeze* works well in lasagna, as a pizza topping, on vegan burgers, stuffed inside cherry tomatoes, in *Zucchini Napoleon* (page 189) or as a sandwich spread. Because of the tahini, it will "melt" *slightly* when cooked, so it works well as a replacement for dairy ricotta in just about any recipe calling for ricotta cheese!

- 1 can (14 to 16 ounces) white kidney beans, drained and rinsed (see note)

- ½ cup water

- 2 tablespoons plus 1 teaspoon sesame tahini

- 1 teaspoon reduced-sodium tamari

- ½ cup chopped raw cashews (see note)

- 1 medium clove garlic, chopped

- ⅛ teaspoon sea salt

Put all of the ingredients into a high-performance blending appliance in the order listed. Process until very smooth in texture, occasionally stopping the machine to scrape down the sides. The *cheeze* will be thick. Covered tightly and refrigerated, the *cheeze* will keep up to 2 days.

CHEF'S NOTES:

- If you do not have white kidney beans, you may use any other variety of cooked white beans in this recipe.

- If you prefer, you may soak the cashews first. To do so, put the cashews into a small bowl and pour water over to cover. Refrigerate for 1 to 4 hours. Drain, rinse and proceed with the recipe as directed.

Tofu-Cashew Whipped Cream

MAKES ABOUT 2 ⅓ CUPS

Pipe this delightful dairy free whipped topping on any dessert or baked sweet treat. This "cream" is also delicious served over a warm bowl of freshly baked granola.

- 1 cup raw cashews
- ¼ cup water, plus more as needed
- ½ block (7 to 8 ounces) firm regular tofu, drained
- 3 tablespoons maple syrup
- 1 teaspoon vanilla extract

Put the cashews into a small bowl and cover with water by ½ inch. Refrigerate and let soak for 1 to 4 hours. Drain the cashews and rinse with cool water.

Put ¼ cup water, the soaked and drained cashews, tofu, maple syrup and vanilla into a high-performance blending appliance, and blend until smooth and creamy, adding more water if needed to achieve the desired consistency. Refrigerate 2 to 4 hours, or until well chilled.

CHEF'S NOTE: If a *soft* and *thin* whipped cream consistency is desired, add an additional ¼ cup water before blending.

78

Vanilla Dessert Topping

MAKES ABOUT 1 ⅓ CUPS

Creamy and rich, this dessert topping whips up in just a few minutes to create a lovely vanilla infused delight to enhance any sweet dessert.

- 1 cup raw cashews
- 2 tablespoons maple syrup
- 1 teaspoon vanilla extract
- 4 tablespoons water, plus more as needed

Put all of the ingredients into a blender and process until smooth and creamy, adding more water, as needed, to achieve the desired consistency. Refrigerate 2 to 4 hours, or until well chilled.

Pineapple, Tomato and Fresh Basil Salsa

MAKES 4 TO 6 SERVINGS

- ½ medium pineapple, peeled, cored and diced

- 2 cups cherry or grape tomatoes, sliced in half

- 1 clove garlic, minced

- 2 tablespoons chopped fresh basil

- ¼ teaspoon sea salt

- Freshly ground black pepper, to taste

Delightfully refreshing, this unique combination of fresh ingredients makes a festive addition to salads, cooked grains, tofu, tempeh or seitan. Use as a bruschetta topping, too!

Put all of the ingredients into a medium-sized bowl and gently stir to combine. Cover and refrigerate at least 1 hour before serving, to allow flavors to marry.

....

All-Purpose Seasoning

MAKES ABOUT 4 ½ TABLESPOONS

I receive *tons* of emails every season inquiring, "What is *All Purpose Seasoning?*" This savvy seasoning is a blend of dried herbs and spices that can be used to enhance many recipes, making recipe prep time quicker and easier. Use it to flavor pasta, casseroles, chili, soups, salads, dips, pizzas, tofu scrambles and so much more. Feel free to add or subtract your favorite dried herbs and spices to create a customized version of this handy and versatile seasoning! You can use this delicious blend any time a recipe in this book calls for *All-Purpose Seasoning*.

- 2 tablespoons dried parsley

- 2 teaspoons dried basil leaves

- 2 teaspoons dried oregano

- 1 teaspoon dried marjoram

- 1 teaspoon garlic powder

- ½ teaspoon onion powder

- ½ teaspoon dried thyme leaves

- ¼ teaspoon celery powder (optional) (see note)

- ⅛ teaspoon dried rubbed sage

- ¹⁄₁₆ teaspoon ground coriander or coriander powder

Put all of the ingredients into a small bowl and stir to thoroughly combine. Transfer to a small jar, cover tightly and store in a dark, dry place.

CHEF'S NOTE: To add a touch of salt to your seasoning, substitute celery salt for the celery powder.

Laura's Italian Seasoning Blend

Here's an economical way to have a quick Italian-style seasoning at your fingertips. Feel free to add your favorite dried herbs to create your own tasty blend. You can use this flavorsome blend anytime a recipe in this book calls for *Italian Seasoning Blend*.

- 1 tablespoon dried basil
- 2½ teaspoons dried oregano
- 1½ teaspoons dried marjoram
- ½ teaspoon dried thyme
- ½ teaspoon dried rosemary
- ¼ teaspoon dried rubbed sage

Put all of the ingredients into a small bowl and stir to thoroughly combine. Transfer to a small jar, cover tightly and store in a dark, dry place.

80

Spicy Italian Seasoning

MAKES 3 TABLESPOONS PLUS 2 TEASPOONS

For folks who are not fond of oregano, this simple, spicy Italian-style seasoning is oregano-free but full of fabulous flavor.

- 4 teaspoons dried basil
- 4 teaspoons dried marjoram
- 4 teaspoons dried parsley
- 1 teaspoon dried rubbed sage
- 1 teaspoon crushed red pepper

Put all of the ingredients into a small bowl and stir to thoroughly combine. Transfer to a small jar, cover tightly and store in a dark, dry place.

CHEF'S NOTES:
- If you prefer a non-spicy seasoning, omit the crushed red pepper.
- If you prefer the taste of oregano in your Italian seasoning, add 2 teaspoons dried oregano.

Jazzy Sazón

MAKES 2 ¾ TABLESPOONS

Spicy Rice (page 233)

- 2 teaspoons ground coriander
- 2 teaspoons ground cumin
- 2 teaspoons smoked paprika
- 1 teaspoon garlic powder
- 1 teaspoon sea salt
- ½ teaspoon dried oregano
- ¼ teaspoon cayenne pepper

This *jazzylicious* seasoning blend enhances soups, stews, casseroles, grains, roasted or grilled vegetables and so much more! Use it in *Spicy Rice* (page 233), *Zesty Maple Almonds* (page 60) or *Vegan Garbanzo Stew* (page 208).

Put all of the ingredients into a small bowl and stir to thoroughly combine. Transfer to a small jar, cover tightly and store in a dark, dry place.

CHAPTER SIX
Marvelous Muffins and Quick Breads

Any time is the right time for baked goods! From moist muffins to simple breads, eye opening coffee cakes and breakfast bars, these vegan treats will satisfy, dazzle and delight, no matter what time of day you serve 'em. Let's get baking!

Recipes

Fabulous Flax-Oat Muffins

MAKES 6 JUMBO MUFFINS

These muffins are a delicious breakfast treat for any morning. Whole wheat flour combined with rolled oats and cornmeal provide the base taste, while ground flaxseeds, dried coconut and plump raisins add moisture and flavor. Deee-lish!

- 4 tablespoons golden flaxseeds
- 1 cup whole wheat flour
- 1 cup fine grind cornmeal
- ½ cup rolled oats
- 2 teaspoons baking powder
- ½ cup unsweetened shredded dried coconut
- ½ cup brown sugar, sucanat or your preferred dry sweetener
- 1¾ cups plus one tablespoon nondairy milk, plus more as needed
- 1 teaspoon vanilla extract
- ½ cup raisins

CHEF'S NOTES:
- You may use a 6-cup standard muffin tin for this recipe to achieve a classic "muffin-top" shape.
- To reheat, preheat the oven to 375 degrees F. Wrap a muffin in foil and warm in the oven for about 20 minutes, or until the muffin is softened and heated through.

Preheat the oven to 375 degrees F. Coat a 6-cup jumbo muffin tin with vegan margarine (see note). Put the flaxseeds into a high-performance blending appliance and process into fine flour.

Put the flax flour, whole wheat flour, cornmeal, rolled oats and baking powder into a large bowl and stir with a dry whisk to combine. Add the coconut and sugar and stir with the whisk to combine. Stir in the nondairy milk and the vanilla extract. Stir in the raisins. The batter will be quite thick, but if it seems overly dry, stir in a bit more nondairy milk, 1 tablespoon at a time, until all of the flour is thoroughly moistened.

Mound the batter into the prepared muffin cups. Smooth out the tops of the muffins with a small rubber spatula. Bake for 30 to 35 minutes, or until golden and a toothpick inserted into the middle of a muffin comes out clean.

Put the muffin tin on a wire rack and loosen the sides of the muffins with a knife. Let cool for about 5 minutes. Carefully remove the muffins from the muffin tin, and let cool for 5 to 10 minutes. Serve warm (see note). Stored tightly covered in the refrigerator, the muffins will keep for up to 2 days.

Maple-Coconut Muffins with Sweet Grape Filling

MAKES 12 MUFFINS

These tasty and moist muffins include a surprise filling, with a sweet pop of grape jelly in every bite!

- 1½ cups whole wheat flour
- ½ cup unsweetened shredded dried coconut
- 1½ teaspoons baking powder
- ½ teaspoon baking soda
- 2 medium ripe bananas
- ⅓ cup maple syrup
- 2 tablespoons extra-virgin olive oil
- 1 teaspoon vanilla extract
- 1 cup unsweetened nondairy milk
- 12 heaping teaspoons grape jelly

Preheat the oven to 375 degrees F. Line a 12-cup standard muffin tin with paper liners.

Put the flour, coconut, baking powder and baking soda into a large bowl and stir with a dry whisk to combine.

Put the bananas, maple syrup, olive oil and vanilla into a medium-sized bowl and mash using a potato masher or large fork until almost smooth. Add the mashed banana mixture and the nondairy milk to the dry ingredients and stir until combined.

Fill each prepared muffin cup two-thirds full with the batter. Make a small well in the center with a spoon or your finger. Spoon 1 heaping teaspoon of grape jelly into the well. Top with the remaining batter, distributing it evenly among the muffin cups. Smooth out the top of each muffin with a rubber spatula.

Bake for 18 to 20 minutes, or until golden and a toothpick inserted into the side of a muffin comes out clean. Put the pan on a wire rack and loosen the sides of each muffin with a knife. Let cool for 20 minutes. Carefully remove the muffins. Serve warm or at room temperature. Covered tightly and stored in the refrigerator, leftover muffins will keep for about 2 days.

Lemony Maple-Cranberry Muffins

MAKES 12 MUFFINS

With the tangy taste of lemon and dried cranberries, enhanced with sweet maple syrup and a dash of wheat germ (for extra added nutrition), this lovely muffin is totally tasty!

- 1¼ cups nondairy milk
- ¼ cup freshly squeezed lemon juice (from about 2 medium lemons; zest the lemons first, before squeezing)
- 2 cups whole wheat flour
- ⅓ cup toasted wheat germ
- 1½ teaspoons baking powder
- ½ teaspoon baking soda
- ½ teaspoon lemon zest
- ⅔ cup firmly packed dark brown sugar
- ¼ cup maple syrup
- ¼ cup water
- 1 tablespoon extra-virgin olive oil
- ½ cup sweetened dried cranberries

Preheat the oven to 375 degrees F. Liberally coat a 12-cup standard muffin tin with vegan margarine. Put the nondairy milk and the lemon juice into a small bowl or pitcher, and let stand while preparing the batter.

To make the batter, put the flour, wheat germ, baking powder and baking soda into a large bowl and stir with a dry whisk until combined. Add the lemon zest and stir with the whisk to combine. Add the brown sugar and briskly whisk to combine. (There will be little flecks of the brown sugar still visible in the flour mixture, but that is fine).

Add the maple syrup, water, olive oil and nondairy milk/lemon mixture, and stir with a large spoon to combine. Fold the cranberries into the batter.

Divide the batter evenly among the 12 muffin cups. Bake for 25 minutes, or until a toothpick inserted into the center of a muffin comes out clean. Put the muffin tin on a wire rack and loosen the sides of the muffins with a knife. Let the muffins cool for 10 minutes. Carefully remove the muffins and put them directly on the wire rack. Let cool 5 minutes and serve. Covered tightly and stored in the refrigerator, leftover muffins will keep for about 3 days.

Glorious Morning Muffins

MAKES 6 JUMBO MUFFINS

Packed with good things like apples, bananas, walnuts, cranberries, carrots and ground flaxseeds, these marvelous muffins make a "power-up" breakfast treat or after school snack.

- 3 tablespoons flaxseeds
- ½ cup walnut halves
- ⅓ cup unsweetened shredded dried coconut
- 1 cup whole wheat flour
- 2 teaspoons baking powder
- 1 cup sliced bananas
- 1⅓ cups peeled, cored and diced apples
- ½ cup maple syrup
- 1 teaspoon ground cinnamon
- ⅓ cup sweetened dried cranberries
- ⅓ cup raisins
- 1 cup shredded carrots (peeling is optional)

Preheat the oven to 375 degrees F. Lightly coat a 6-cup jumbo muffin tin with vegan margarine.

Put the flaxseeds into a high-performance blending appliance and process into fine flour. Add the walnuts and coconut and process into coarse flour. Transfer to a large bowl. Add the whole wheat flour and baking powder and stir with a dry whisk to combine.

Put the bananas, apples, maple syrup and cinnamon into a blender and process until smooth. Add the banana mixture to the flour and stir with a large spoon to make a batter. Fold in the cranberries and raisins and mix just until incorporated. Fold in the shredded carrots and gently mix just until incorporated. Divide the batter among the muffin cups.

Bake for 28 to 30 minutes. Check the muffins, and if the tops are browning too quickly, tent loosely with foil. Bake an additional 8 to 10 minutes, or until golden and tops of the muffins are quite firm to the touch. Put the pan on a wire rack and loosen the sides of each muffin with a knife. Let cool for 12 to 15 minutes. Carefully remove the muffins. Serve warm or at room temperature. Covered tightly and stored in the refrigerator, leftover muffins will keep for about 2 days.

Four-Ingredient Apricot Bars

MAKES 12 BARS

These tasty bars are easy to make, while being easy on the wallet. The sweetness comes from the apricot preserves, and rolled oats provide the crunch. Mashed bananas stand in beautifully for the egg, and the vanilla extract really jazzes it up!

- 2 medium ripe bananas, peeled and sliced

- 1 teaspoon vanilla extract

- 1½ cups plus 1 tablespoon rolled oats

- ¾ cup thick apricot preserves (see note)

Preheat the oven to 375 degrees F. Lightly coat an 8-inch square rimmed baking pan with vegan margarine. Line the pan with unbleached parchment paper, leaving an overhang of 2-inch "wings" on two opposite sides of the pan.

To make the dough, put the bananas and the vanilla extract into a large bowl and mash into a chunky purée, using a potato masher or large fork. Add the oats and stir with a large spoon to thoroughly combine.

Press half of the dough mixture into the prepared pan in an even layer. Spread the apricot preserves over the dough in an even layer. Top with the remaining dough, patting it down gently into an even layer.

Bake for 22 to 25 minutes, or until the edges are golden. Put the pan on a wire rack and let cool 15 minutes. Cut the "cake" into 12 bars, using a serrated knife and wiping the knife clean often. Using the paper "wings," carefully lift the bars out of the pan and set them on the wire rack. Let the bars cool for 10 to 20 minutes before serving. Wrapped tightly and refrigerated, leftover bars will keep up to 2 days.

CHEF'S NOTE: If the preserves you are using are "watery," drain the excess liquid from the preserves before measuring and using in this recipe. Do this by placing the preserves in a fine-screened sieve set over a bowl. Let drain for 15 minutes. Proceed with recipe as directed.

Almond, Oat and Fruit Bars

MAKES 12 BARS

Not too sweet, but full of fabulous flavors, these gooey *and* crunchy bars make a satisfying snack, plus they do double-duty as a healthy dessert!

- ½ cup raw almonds
- 1 cup whole wheat flour
- 1 cup rolled oats
- 1 teaspoon ground cinnamon
- ½ teaspoon baking powder
- ¼ cup cold vegan margarine
- ¼ cup maple syrup
- 3 tablespoons brown sugar
- 3 tablespoons cold nondairy milk
- ⅓ cup plus 3 tablespoons apricot, raspberry or blueberry preserves (see note on page 92)

Preheat the oven to 375 degrees F. Lightly coat an 8-inch square rimmed baking pan with vegan margarine. Line the pan with unbleached parchment paper, leaving an overhang of 2-inch "wings" on two opposite sides of the pan.

Put the almonds into a blender and process into coarse flour. Transfer the almond flour to a large bowl. Add the flour, oats, cinnamon and baking powder and stir with a dry whisk to combine. Add the vegan margarine, maple syrup, brown sugar and cold nondairy milk, and mix using a dough blender or fork, until the dough forms pea-size pieces. Gather the dough up with your hands and gently knead it in the bowl for about 10 seconds, until it comes together.

Press half of the dough into the prepared pan in an even layer. Spread the preserves in an even layer over the dough. Top with the remaining dough, patting it down gently into an even layer.

Bake for 20 to 25 minutes, or until the edges of the bars are golden. Put the pan on a wire rack and let cool 3 minutes. Using the paper "wings," carefully lift the bars out of the pan, and set them on the wire rack. Let cool 10 minutes. Using the paper "wings," transfer to a cutting board and gently slice into 12 bars, using a serrated knife and wiping the knife clean after cutting each bar. Cool 10 minutes before serving. Wrapped tightly and refrigerated, leftover bars will keep up to 2 days.

Lots-a-Lemon Coconut Bars

MAKES 16 BARS

Lots of lemon and coconut make these chewy bars an excellent choice when you crave a citrus-flavored snack!

94

- 1½ cups whole wheat flour

- ½ cup unsweetened shredded dried coconut

- ½ cup plus 1 teaspoon vegan cane sugar, divided

- 1 heaping tablespoon lemon zest (from 1 large lemon)

- ½ teaspoon baking powder

- ¼ cup vegan margarine

- 3 tablespoons maple syrup

- 2½ tablespoons freshly squeezed lemon juice

- 2 tablespoons cold nondairy milk

Preheat the oven to 400 degrees F. Lightly coat an 8-inch square rimmed baking pan with vegan margarine. Line the pan with unbleached parchment paper, leaving an overhang of 2-inch "wings" on two opposite sides of the pan.

Put the flour, coconut, ½ cup sugar, lemon zest and baking powder into a large bowl and stir with a dry whisk to combine. Add the vegan margarine, maple syrup and lemon juice, and mix for about 20 seconds using a dough blender or large fork. Add the cold nondairy milk and continue to combine using the dough blender or fork until the dough forms pea-size pieces.

Gather the dough up with your hands and press it into the prepared pan in an even layer. Using a dinner fork, poke multiple holes in the top of the dough. Score the dough into 16 bars. Sprinkle the remaining 1 teaspoon sugar evenly over the top of the dough.

Bake for 17 to 20 minutes, or until the edges of the bars are golden (the center will still be a bit soft). Put the pan on a wire rack and let cool 1 minute. Using the paper "wings," carefully lift the bars out of the pan and set them on a cutting board. Using a sharp knife, gently cut the dough into 16 bars. Put the bars back on the rack and let cool 15 to 20 minutes before serving. Wrapped tightly and refrigerated, leftover bars will keep up to 2 days.

Chocolate Chip-Oatmeal Bread

MAKES 12 SLICES

Need a treat, but want it to be filling too? This lively bread makes a nutritious indulgence when you're seeking something sweet, but you want health benefits too! With a pop of chocolate nestled in a batter of whole wheat flour, rolled oats, sunflower seeds and raisins, this quick bread will truly satisfy. Serve slathered with your favorite preserves and some nut or seed butter for a light lunch or hearty snack.

- 1½ cups whole wheat flour

- 1 cup plus 1½ tablespoons rolled oats, divided

- 2 teaspoons baking powder

- ⅓ cup vegan cane sugar

- ½ teaspoon ground cinnamon

- ½ cup raisins

- ⅓ cup vegan dark chocolate chips (70% or 85% cacao)

- ⅓ cup raw, unsalted sunflower seeds

- 1½ cups nondairy milk, plus more as needed

Preheat the oven to 375 degrees F. Lightly coat an 8 by 4-inch loaf pan with vegan margarine. Line the lengthwise sides and bottom of the pan with unbleached parchment paper, leaving an overhang of 2-inch "wings" on the two long sides of the pan.

Put the whole wheat flour, 1 cup rolled oats and baking powder into a large bowl, and stir with a dry whisk to combine. Add the sugar and cinnamon, and stir with the whisk to combine. Stir in the raisins, chocolate chips and sunflower seeds, and mix with a large spoon to combine. Add the nondairy milk and stir until well blended, adding a bit more nondairy milk if the mixture seems dry. Batter will be thick.

Spoon the batter into the prepared loaf pan, smoothing the top with a rubber spatula. Sprinkle 1½ tablespoons of rolled oats evenly over the top of the bread. Bake for 40 to 45 minutes, or until the top of the bread is firm, slightly golden and a toothpick inserted in the center of the bread comes out clean.

Put the bread on a wire rack and let cool for 5 minutes. Using the parchment paper "wings," carefully lift the bread from the pan and put it on the wire rack. Carefully peel back the paper from the sides of the bread and let cool an additional 10 to 15 minutes before slicing. Serve warm, or wrap tightly, refrigerate and serve cold. Wrapped tightly and stored in the refrigerator, leftover bread will keep for 3 days.

Banana-Walnut Bread

MAKES 10 TO 12 SLICES

This delicious bread makes a wonderful snack, slathered with a bit of vegan margarine, nut butter or your favorite fruit preserves.

- 1 cup plus 1 tablespoon nondairy milk
- 2 tablespoons freshly squeezed lemon juice
- 2 cups plus 2 tablespoons whole wheat flour
- 1 teaspoon baking soda
- 1 cup vegan cane sugar
- ⅓ cup extra-light olive oil (see note)
- 1 teaspoon vanilla extract
- 1½ cups mashed ripe bananas (about 3 medium)
- 1 cup chopped walnuts

Preheat the oven to 375 degrees F. Lightly coat a 9 by 5-inch loaf pan with vegan margarine. Line the lengthwise sides and bottom of the pan with unbleached parchment paper, leaving an overhang of 2-inch "wings" on the two long sides of the pan.

Put the nondairy milk and lemon juice into a small bowl or pitcher, and stir to combine. Let stand at room temperature while preparing the batter.

Put the flour, baking soda and sugar in a large bowl, and stir with a dry whisk until combined. Add the nondairy milk/lemon juice mixture, oil, vanilla and mashed bananas, and stir with a large spoon until combined. Fold in the chopped walnuts.

Pour the batter into the prepared loaf pan. Bake for 45 minutes. Decrease the heat to 350 degrees F and bake for an additional 15 to 20 minutes, or until the top is golden and a toothpick inserted into the center of the loaf comes out clean.

Put the pan on a wire rack. Lift the bread out of the pan using the paper "wings." Let cool for at least 1 hour before slicing. Wrapped tightly and stored in the refrigerator, leftover bread will keep for 3 days.

CHEF'S NOTE: If desired, you may use extra-virgin olive oil in place of the extra-light olive oil. The bread will be slightly denser in texture.

Zucchini Bread

MAKES 2 LOAVES

- 3 cups whole wheat pastry flour
- 1¼ cups unsweetened shredded dried coconut
- 1 cup rolled oats
- 1 cup sucanat, dark brown sugar or your preferred dry sweetener
- 3 tablespoons plus 1 teaspoon freshly ground golden flaxseeds
- 1 tablespoon baking powder
- ½ teaspoon sea salt
- 2 cups nondairy milk
- 1 cup water
- ¼ cup extra-virgin olive oil
- 3 cups lightly packed grated zucchini
- ⅓ cup raisins
- ⅓ cup sweetened dried cranberries

This nutrient-dense quick bread is easy to prepare, and it stores well in the refrigerator for several days. Rolled oats help the loaf hold together, while ground flaxseeds stand in well for the egg. Coconut contributes a welcome punch of moisture and flavor. So fresh *and* tasty!

Preheat the oven to 350 degrees F. Generously coat two 8 by 4-inch or 9 by 5-inch loaf pans with vegan margarine.

Put the flour, coconut, oats, sucanat (or brown sugar), flaxseeds, baking powder and salt in a large bowl and stir with a dry whisk to combine. Stir in the nondairy milk, water and oil. Fold in the zucchini, raisins and cranberries. Mix just until incorporated. The batter will be thick.

Divide the batter evenly between the two loaf pans and smooth out the top. Bake for 65 to 75 minutes, or until a toothpick inserted into the center of a loaf comes out clean and the tops are slightly golden.

Put the pans on a wire rack and loosen the sides of each loaf with a knife. Let cool for 30 minutes. Carefully invert each pan, and gently remove the loaves. Put the loaves back onto the wire rack. Let cool 10 minutes before slicing. Covered tightly and stored in the refrigerator, leftover bread will keep for about 4 days.

Banana-Pecan Coffee Cake

MAKES 8 TO 10 SERVINGS

Need coffee cake? This easy-to-prepare, enticing baked delight makes a fabulous mid-morning nosh. Laced with creamy ripe bananas, vanilla, sweet cinnamon and crunchy pecans, this cake will do triple-duty as a breakfast treat, afternoon snack or delectable dessert.

- 3 tablespoons golden flaxseeds

- 2 cups whole wheat pastry flour

- ½ cup plus 1 tablespoon vegan cane sugar, divided

- 2 teaspoons ground cinnamon

- 2 teaspoons baking powder

- 3 medium ripe bananas

- 1¼ cups plus 1 tablespoon nondairy milk

- 1 tablespoon maple syrup

- 1 teaspoon vanilla extract

- 1 cup chopped pecans

Preheat the oven to 350 degrees F. Lightly coat a 9 by 9-inch square baking pan with vegan margarine. Line the pan with unbleached parchment paper, leaving an overhang of 2-inch "wings" on two opposite sides of the pan.

Put the flaxseeds into a high-performance blending appliance and process into fine flour. Put the ground flaxseeds, flour, ½ cup sugar, cinnamon and baking powder into a large bowl and stir with a wire whisk to thoroughly combine.

Put the bananas, nondairy milk, maple syrup and vanilla extract into a blender and process for about 30 seconds, until smooth and creamy in texture. Add the banana mixture to the flour mixture and mix together using a large spoon to make a batter, adding more nondairy milk, 1 tablespoon at a time, if batter seems dry. Fold in the pecans.

Pour the batter into the prepared pan and smooth the top. Sprinkle 1 tablespoon sugar evenly over the top of the batter. Bake for 35 to 45 minutes or until a toothpick inserted into the center of the cake comes out clean. Put the pan on a wire rack. Lift the cake out of the pan using the paper "wings." Let cool for 20 to 30 minutes before cutting into squares and serving. Wrapped tightly and stored in the refrigerator, leftover cake will keep for 2 days.

JAZZY TIP: Vanilla extract adds sweetness to baked goods recipes, making it possible to lower the amount of sugar used without sacrificing that sugary taste that we all crave.

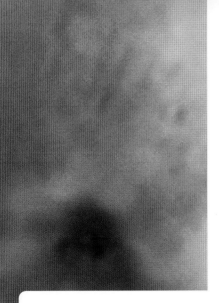

Apple 'n Date Coffee Cake

MAKES 6 SERVINGS

A yummy layer of apples top this tasty cake that's filled with good things like bananas, coconut and sweet dates. It's the perfect snack to complement hot tea or a dark cup o' joe.

APPLE LAYER

- 2 medium apples, cored and diced (do not peel)

- 1 tablespoon brown sugar, sucanat or your preferred dry sweetener

- 1 tablespoon maple syrup

CAKE

- 2 medium ripe bananas

- 1 tablespoon maple syrup

- 1 cup whole wheat flour

- ⅓ cup unsweetened shredded dried coconut

- ¼ cup brown sugar, sucanat or your preferred dry sweetener

- 1 teaspoon baking powder

- ½ cup pitted and diced Medjool or Deglet dates

- ⅔ cup water

Preheat the oven to 375 degrees F. Lightly coat a 9-inch round cake pan with vegan margarine. Line the bottom of the pan with unbleached parchment paper.

To make the apple layer, put the apples, 1 tablespoon brown sugar or sucanat and 1 tablespoon maple syrup into a medium-sized bowl and stir until the apples are evenly coated. Transfer to the prepared pan, spreading the apples in an even layer.

To make the cake batter, put the bananas and maple syrup into a medium-sized bowl, and mash into a chunky purée using a potato masher or large fork.

Put the flour, coconut, ¼ cup brown sugar or sucanat and baking powder into a large bowl and stir with a dry whisk to combine. Stir in the banana mixture, dates and water and mix just until incorporated.

Pour the batter over the apples in the pan and smooth the top. Bake for 40 to 50 minutes, or until golden and a toothpick inserted into the center of the cake comes out clean.

Put the pan on a wire rack and loosen the sides with a knife. Let cool for 10 to 12 minutes. Invert onto a serving platter and carefully peel off the parchment paper. Let cool for 5 minutes more before slicing. Wrapped tightly and refrigerated, leftover cake will keep for about 3 days.

CHAPTER SEVEN

The Daily Green

L et's face it. Sometimes eating your daily salad can seem like a chore, so I'm sharing some of my favorite ways to serve up your dose of greens to make 'em totally tasty!

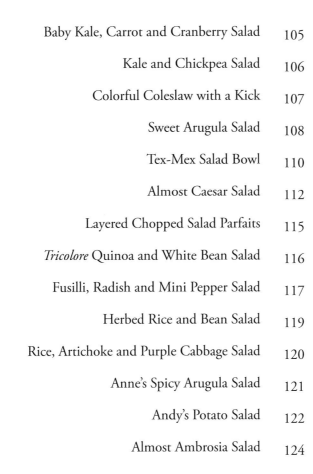

Recipes

Festive Kale-Cranberry Salad

Baby Kale, Carrot and Cranberry Salad

If you crave greens, this is the salad for you. The mild taste of baby kale is pleasing, while the maple syrup, carrots and cranberries provide a bit of sweet. This combo is delightful to serve as a first course for a dinner party, but I also love to serve it for a luncheon side salad.

DRESSING

- 3 tablespoons freshly squeezed lemon juice
- 2 tablespoons maple syrup
- ½ clove garlic, minced

SALAD

- 8 cups lightly packed baby kale, stems removed and roughly chopped
- 1 cup grated carrots (peeling is optional)
- ½ cup sweetened dried cranberries
- ½ cup chopped walnuts or pecans

Put all of the dressing ingredients into a small bowl and whisk until thoroughly combined.

Put the kale into a large bowl and, using clean hands, gently massage to break down the tough fibers. Add the carrots, cranberries and walnuts or pecans. Pour the dressing over the salad and toss gently until thoroughly combined. Serve immediately, or cover and refrigerate for up to 3 hours before serving.

VARIATIONS:

- **Baby Kale, Carrot and Cherry Salad** – Substitute dried cherries for the sweetened dried cranberries.
- **Festive Kale-Cranberry Salad** – Omit the garlic and carrots and substitute thinly sliced curly kale for the baby kale. For a sweeter dressing, add 1 more tablespoon of maple syrup.

Kale and Chickpea Salad

MAKES 4 TO 6 SERVINGS

- 1 can (15 to 16 ounces) chickpeas (garbanzo beans), drained and rinsed
- 2 cups firmly packed curly kale, stems removed and *very* thinly sliced
- 3 tablespoons freshly squeezed lemon juice
- 1 tablespoon plus 1 teaspoon extra-virgin olive oil
- 1 tablespoon maple syrup
- 2 medium cloves garlic, minced
- 1 teaspoon Italian seasoning blend
- ¼ teaspoon sea salt
- Several grinds of freshly ground black pepper, to taste
- 20 to 24 grape or cherry tomatoes, sliced in half
- 12 Kalamata olives, pitted and chopped
- ½ cup peeled and diced cucumber
- 2 medium carrots, grated (peeling is optional)

With a little bit of crunch from carrots, kale and cucumbers, and a whole lot of deliciousness from hearty chickpeas, this unique salad makes a great centerpiece for a ladies' luncheon or a first course salad for a celebratory meal.

Put the chickpeas, kale, lemon juice, olive oil, maple syrup, garlic, Italian seasoning, salt and pepper into a large bowl and stir with a large spoon to thoroughly combine. Let the mixture stand for 10 minutes to allow flavors to marry.

Add the tomatoes, olives, cucumber and carrots to the salad, and gently toss using a large spoon to thoroughly coat. Cover loosely and refrigerate for 1 hour, or up to 4 hours, and serve.

Colorful Coleslaw with a Kick

MAKES 6 SERVINGS

- 4 cups white cabbage, thinly sliced

- 4 cups purple (red) cabbage, thinly sliced

- 2 large (or 3 medium) carrots, peeled and grated

- 5 heaping tablespoons vegan mayonnaise, plus more as needed

- 2 tablespoons Dijon mustard

- 1 tablespoon maple syrup

- 1 teaspoon Italian seasoning blend

- ½ teaspoon garlic powder

- ¼ teaspoon smoked paprika

- ⅛ teaspoon cayenne pepper

- ¼ teaspoon sea salt

- Freshly ground black pepper, to taste

My husband calls this "hot" slaw because it has a good bit of spice to it, and it's super satisfying!

Put the white cabbage, purple (red) cabbage and carrots into a large bowl.

To make the dressing, put the mayonnaise, Dijon mustard, maple syrup, Italian seasoning, garlic powder, smoked paprika and cayenne pepper into a small bowl. Briskly whisk until smooth.

Pour the dressing over the cabbage and carrot mixture, and stir with a large spoon until well combined. Taste and add more mayonnaise, if desired. Add sea salt and freshly ground pepper, to taste. Cover and refrigerate for at least 1 hour, or up to 6 hours, before serving.

Sweet Arugula Salad

MAKES 2 TO 4 SERVINGS

A sweet dressing paired with tangy dried cranberries, crisp Granny Smith apples and spicy arugula makes a tempting salad combination.

SALAD

- 5 ounces baby arugula, washed and dried
- 1 medium orange or red sweet bell pepper, seeded and chopped
- 1 small Granny Smith apple, peeled, cored and chopped
- ⅓ cup sweetened dried cranberries
- ⅓ cup roasted unsalted almonds

DRESSING

- 2 tablespoons freshly squeezed lemon juice
- 2 tablespoons maple syrup
- 1 teaspoon extra-virgin olive oil
- 1 teaspoon balsamic vinegar
- Sea salt, to taste
- Freshly ground black pepper, to taste

Put all of the salad ingredients into a large bowl and gently toss with large tongs to combine.

Put all of the dressing ingredients in a small bowl and briskly whisk to emulsify.

Pour the dressing over the salad and gently toss to coat. Serve immediately.

Tex-Mex Salad Bowl

MAKES 2 MAIN DISH SALADS

This *Tex-Mex* style salad features a zingy lime-based dressing, paired with crisp romaine and cooked garbanzo beans. But since a *Tex-Mex* style salad is traditionally made with black beans, I decided to add a jazzy twist by substituting black bean tortilla chips as a festive garnish. The chips provide a pleasing crunch, flavor and texture, adding a *wow* factor to this satisfying salad.

SALAD

- 8 cups loosely packed baby romaine or chopped romaine
- 20 black bean tortilla chips
- 14 grape or cherry tomatoes, sliced in half
- 1 cup cooked chickpeas (garbanzo beans), drained and rinsed, if canned
- Kernels from 1 large ear of corn, cooked (or ¾ cup canned corn kernels, drained)
- ½ cup seeded and chopped orange or red sweet bell pepper
- 4 green queen olives with pimento, sliced
- ½ of a large avocado, peeled, pitted and sliced

SWEET AND SPICY LIME DRESSING

- 2½ tablespoons vegan mayonnaise
- 1 tablespoon freshly squeezed lime juice
- 1 tablespoon maple syrup
- 1/16 teaspoon cayenne pepper

For each salad, put 4 cups of lettuce into a large bowl. Arrange 10 tortilla chips around the circumference of the bowl. Artfully arrange 14 tomato halves on top of the lettuce. Top with one-half of the chickpeas, corn kernels and sweet peppers. Sprinkle one-half of the olives over the salad and arrange one-half of the avocado slices on top in a pleasing manner.

Put all of the dressing ingredients into a small bowl and briskly whisk until smooth (see note). Drizzle one-half of the dressing over each salad, and serve.

CHEF'S NOTE: For a creamier dressing, add more mayonnaise (up to 2 tablespoons), to taste.

JAZZY TIP: Squeeze fresh lime or lemon juice over cut avocados to help keep the edges from turning brown. Plus, the citrus will infuse the avocado with a welcome punch of vibrant flavor!

Almost Caesar Salad

MAKES 2 TO 4 SERVINGS

- ½ cup water
- ⅓ cup plus 3 tablespoons walnut pieces, divided
- 1 tablespoon freshly squeezed lemon juice
- ½ tablespoon capers, drained
- 1 teaspoon Dijon mustard
- Sea salt, to taste
- Freshly ground black pepper, to taste
- 1 medium head romaine lettuce, washed, dried and torn into bite-sized pieces

The creamy dressing in this salad is reminiscent of the classic version but takes less than 3 minutes to make! Processing the walnuts with a few flavorful ingredients offers a wonderful egg-like texture, while the capers stand in beautifully for anchovies. Give it a try—you'll be glad you did.

Put the water, ⅓ cup walnuts, lemon juice, capers and Dijon mustard into a blender and process until smooth and creamy in texture. Add salt and pepper, to taste. Put the lettuce into a large bowl. Pour the dressing over the lettuce and toss gently until evenly coated. Garnish with the remaining 3 tablespoons walnuts. Serve at once.

112

Layered Chopped Salad Parfaits

These beautiful parfaits taste as good as they look. With layered crisp veggies, zingy olives and crunchy walnuts, all topped with a *Cream-a-licious Dressing* (page 67), this festive chopped salad will surely be a hit at your next soirée.

SALAD

- 3 cups finely chopped romaine lettuce

- 1½ cups finely chopped tomatoes

- 1 cup seeded and finely chopped orange or red sweet bell pepper

- ½ cup seeded and chopped cucumber

- ½ cup finely chopped walnuts

- ½ cup finely chopped green olives with pimento (see note)

DRESSING

- *Cream-a-licious Dressing* (page 67)

CHEF'S NOTE: You may use Kalamata olives in place of the green variety, if desired.

Put about ¼ cup of lettuce in each of four large (12-ounce) parfait glasses or bowls. Drizzle about 1 teaspoon of the dressing over the lettuce in each of the four glasses.

Layer about 2 tablespoons of tomatoes and 2 tablespoons of peppers on top of the lettuce/dressing layer. Drizzle about 1 teaspoon of the dressing over the tomato/pepper layer in each of the four glasses.

Top with about ¼ cup of lettuce, 2 tablespoons of cucumbers, 2 more tablespoons of tomatoes and 1 tablespoon of walnuts. Drizzle about 1 teaspoon of the dressing over the cucumber/tomato/walnut layer in each of the four glasses.

Top with 2 tablespoons of peppers, about ¼ cup of lettuce, 2 tablespoons of olives and 1 tablespoon of walnuts. Garnish each parfait with about 2 tablespoons of tomatoes. Drizzle about 1 teaspoon of the dressing over the top of the salad, in each of the four glasses. Refrigerate for 20 to 30 minutes before serving, to let the flavors marry.

Tricolore Quinoa and White Bean Salad

MAKES 6 SERVINGS

SALAD

- 1½ cups *tricolore* or white quinoa, rinsed thoroughly and drained
- 3 cups water
- 1 medium cucumber, peeled, seeded and diced
- 3 medium carrots, diced (peeling is optional)
- 2 cups chopped tomatoes
- 1¼ cups pitted Kalamata olives, diced
- 1 can (15 to 16 ounces) Great Northern white beans, drained and rinsed

. . . .

DRESSING

- 3 tablespoons freshly squeezed lemon juice (see note)
- 3 tablespoons extra-virgin olive oil
- 2 teaspoons tamari
- 2 teaspoons Italian seasoning blend
- 1 teaspoon maple syrup
- ¼ teaspoon ground turmeric
- 2 small cloves garlic, minced
- Sea salt, to taste
- Freshly ground black pepper, to taste

Serve this high-protein salad over a bed of crisp romaine for a simple but satisfying one-dish meal.

Put the quinoa and water into a medium-sized saucepan and bring to a boil over medium heat. Decrease the heat to medium-low, cover and simmer for 15 to 17 minutes, or until all of the liquid is absorbed. Fluff with a fork, remove from heat, cover and let stand for 10 minutes. Transfer to a large bowl and let cool (see note).

Once the quinoa has cooled, add the cucumber, carrots, tomatoes, olives and white beans, and gently stir with a large spoon to combine.

Put all of the dressing ingredients into a small bowl and briskly whisk until emulsified. Pour the dressing over the quinoa mixture and gently toss to thoroughly coat. Season with sea salt and freshly ground pepper, to taste. Cover and refrigerate for 2 to 4 hours to allow the flavors to marry. Before serving, taste and add more sea salt and/or freshly ground black pepper, if desired (see note).

CHEF'S NOTES:

- For a more pronounced lemon flavor, add an additional 1 tablespoon of lemon juice to the dressing.
- The quinoa may be cooked up to 24 hours in advance and stored in the refrigerator before using in this recipe.
- To add a pop of freshness, stir in either ½ cup chopped fresh flat leaf parsley or ½ cup chopped fresh basil to the salad before serving.

116

Fusilli, Radish and Mini Pepper Salad

MAKES 6 SERVINGS

SALAD

- 1 pound cooked and cooled fusilli, penne or macaroni (or your favorite pasta variety)
- 1¼ cups diced celery, with leaves
- 1 cup diced carrots (peeling is optional)
- ¾ cup chopped red radishes
- 1½ cups sweet mini peppers, cut into thin rings
- ⅔ cup plus 1 tablespoon diced green olives with pimento
- 1 cup cooked chickpeas (garbanzo beans), drained and rinsed, if canned

DRESSING

- ¼ cup plus 2 tablespoons vegan mayonnaise, plus more as needed
- 2 tablespoons Dijon mustard, plus more as needed
- 1 tablespoon Italian seasoning blend
- 2 teaspoons maple syrup
- Sea salt, to taste
- Freshly ground black pepper, to taste

SERVING SUGGESTION

- 6 cups chopped romaine lettuce
- 12 to 18 cherry tomatoes, sliced in half
- 3 to 4 large red radishes, thinly sliced

This tempting pasta salad gets jazzy pizzazz from spicy red radishes and sweet mini peppers. Serve this tasty, cold pasta dish any time a hearty summer salad is required.

Put the cooked and cooled fusilli, celery, carrots, radish, peppers, olives and chickpeas into a large bowl and gently stir with a large spoon to combine.

To make the dressing, put the mayonnaise, Dijon mustard, Italian seasoning and maple syrup in a small bowl and briskly whisk until smooth. Pour the dressing over the salad and gently stir to thoroughly coat. Season with salt and pepper, to taste. Cover and refrigerate for 3 to 4 hours, or until thoroughly chilled. Serve in a large bowl (family style) or on individual serving plates spooned over a bed of chopped romaine lettuce and garnished with cherry tomatoes and radish slices, if desired.

Herbed Rice and Bean Salad

MAKES 4 TO 6 SERVINGS

SALAD

- 2½ cups cooked long grain brown rice
- 1 can (15 to 16 ounces) chickpeas (garbanzo beans), drained and rinsed
- 1¼ cup grape or cherry tomatoes, sliced in half
- 1 cup diced celery, with leaves
- ½ cup seeded and diced red or orange sweet bell pepper
- 1 small onion, diced
- 1 cup diced purple (red) cabbage
- 6 tablespoons capers, drained and rinsed
- 2 large fresh sage leaves, minced
- 2 tablespoons minced fresh parsley, plus more for garnish
- 1 tablespoon minced fresh basil

DRESSING

- 2½ tablespoons freshly squeezed lemon juice, plus more as needed
- 1 heaping tablespoon Dijon mustard
- 1 tablespoon maple syrup
- 1 tablespoon extra-virgin olive oil
- 1 clove garlic, minced
- ¼ teaspoon sea salt, plus more to taste
- Several grinds of freshly ground black pepper, plus more to taste

GARNISH

- ¼ teaspoon sweet paprika
- Parsley sprigs

Leftover rice? Rejoice! This is the perfect way to incorporate cooked brown rice into a super sassy summer salad. The chickpeas provide a pop of protein, while a rainbow of veggies add vibrant color and tantalizing texture. For entertaining purposes, you can make this salad well ahead of time and refrigerate until serving, so it's ideal for serving at a warm weather get-together!

Put all of the salad ingredients into a large bowl and stir with a large spoon to combine. Put all of the dressing ingredients into a small bowl and briskly whisk to combine.

Pour the dressing over the salad and gently toss to coat. Taste and add more lemon juice, if desired, and season with more salt and pepper if needed. Sprinkle paprika over the top.

Serve in a large bowl (family style), or divide into four to six pasta "style" serving bowls and garnish with parsley sprigs.

SALAD

- 3 cups cooked and chilled brown rice
- 2 cups lightly packed and *very* finely chopped kale, remove stems before chopping
- 2 cups lightly packed, finely chopped purple (red) cabbage
- 1 cup drained and chopped water-packed artichoke hearts
- 1 cup thinly sliced celery

DRESSING

- 2 heaping tablespoons vegan mayonnaise
- 1 heaping tablespoon Dijon mustard
- 1 teaspoon maple syrup
- 1 teaspoon all-purpose seasoning
- ¼ teaspoon sea salt
- ⅛ teaspoon cayenne pepper

Rice, Artichoke and Purple Cabbage Salad

MAKES 4 SERVINGS

This unique combination of tastes and textures provides a welcome change to your luncheon salad. My husband loves this mixture of nutty brown rice, tangy artichokes and crisp cabbage, and I think you will too!

Put all of the salad ingredients into a large bowl and gently stir to combine.

Put all of the dressing ingredients into a small bowl and briskly whisk to combine. Pour the dressing over the salad and gently toss to coat. Serve at once, or cover and refrigerate for 2 hours or up to 6 hours prior to serving.

CHEF'S NOTE : A trio of brown, red and black rice is great to use in this recipe.

Anne's Spicy Arugula Salad

MAKES 4 SERVINGS

SALAD

- 4 cups very firmly packed baby arugula
- 1 medium tomato, diced
- ½ medium red onion, thinly sliced

DRESSING

- 2 tablespoons extra-virgin olive oil
- ½ tablespoon finely chopped spring onion, white part only (optional)
- 1 tablespoon freshly squeezed lime juice
- 1 teaspoon maple syrup
- Dash of cayenne pepper

GARNISH (optional)

- Zesty Maple Almonds (page 60)

Our talented culinary supervisor for Season Six of *Jazzy Vegetarian* created this fabulously fresh and delicious salad that pairs perfectly with almost any meal. Try serving it with *Seitan Fajitas* (page 198), *Black Bean-Zucchini Burritos* (page 210) or *Asparagus Tart* (page 146).

Put all of the salad ingredients into a large bowl and gently toss with large tongs to combine.

Put all of the dressing ingredients in a small bowl and briskly whisk to emulsify. Pour the dressing over the salad and toss with the tongs to coat. Garnish with *Zesty Maple Almonds* (page 60), if desired. Serve immediately.

Andy's Potato Salad

MAKES 6 SERVINGS

My husband *loves* this potato salad, so I just *had* to name it after him. A real crowd-pleaser, this tasty dish incorporates tender red potatoes, combined with crisp carrots and crunchy celery, all smothered in a sassy vegan mayonnaise dressing.

SALAD

- 9 cups cubed red potatoes, cut into 1-inch pieces
- 5 medium carrots, peeled and diced
- 4 medium stalks celery, with leaves, diced
- ¾ cup queen green olives with pimento, diced (see note)

DRESSING

- 6 tablespoons vegan mayonnaise, plus more as needed
- 3 tablespoons Dijon mustard, plus more as needed
- 1 teaspoon maple syrup
- 1 teaspoon dried parsley, or 1 tablespoon chopped fresh parsley
- ½ teaspoon dried basil, or 1½ tablespoons chopped fresh basil
- ¼ teaspoon sea salt, plus more as needed
- Freshly ground black pepper, to taste

Fit a steamer basket into a large pot with a tight-fitting lid. Add 2 to 3 inches of cold water, then add the red potatoes. Cover, bring to a boil and steam 25 minutes or until fork tender. Transfer the potatoes to a large bowl and let cool about 30 minutes (see note). Add the carrots, celery and olives to the potatoes, and gently stir to combine.

Put all of the dressing ingredients into a small bowl and briskly whisk to combine. Pour the dressing over the potato mixture and gently stir to thoroughly coat. Add more vegan mayonnaise and/or Dijon mustard, to taste, if the salad seems dry.

Taste and add more salt and several grinds of black pepper, if desired. Cover and refrigerate for at least 3 hours, or up to 24 hours before serving. The dressing will be absorbed into the potatoes as the salad chills, so if it seems dry, right before serving, add more vegan mayonnaise and/or Dijon mustard, to taste.

CHEF'S NOTES:

· You may use black olives or pitted Kalamata olives in place of the green olives, if desired.

· You may cook the potatoes in advance, cover and refrigerate them for up to 12 hours before preparing the recipe.

Almost Ambrosia Salad

MAKES 2 TO 4 SERVINGS

"Yum!" is all I can say about this truly satisfying fruit salad. Reminiscent of a classic ambrosia, but sans the overly sweet marshmallows, this lively dish is great to serve for a morning treat but also works well as a first course for an elegant dinner party.

- 2 clementines, divided into sections
- 1½ cups peeled, cored and cubed pineapple
- 1 very large or 2 small bananas, sliced
- 2 tablespoons unsweetened shredded dried coconut
- 4 large Medjool dates, pitted and chopped

Squeeze the juice from 3 or 4 of the clementine sections into the bottom of a medium-sized bowl. Add the remaining clementine sections, pineapple, banana, coconut and dates to the bowl. Gently toss to combine. Divide into 2 to 4 pretty dishes, and serve.

CHAPTER EIGHT

Soup's On!

S oup's On! That's what my husband likes to hear any time of day or year. With satisfying veggie soups, bean-based potages and refreshing chilled options, the recipes in this chapter are sure to make your family come running to the table!

Recipes

Minty Cucumber and Carrot Soup

MAKES 4 SERVINGS

This chilled soup makes a colorful and refreshing first course, or a light and frosty summertime luncheon entrée. The beautiful orange hue, combined with a hint of mint, produces a delicate and welcoming flavor to this easy to make warm weather soup.

- 2⅔ cups peeled, seeded and chopped cucumber
- 1½ cups peeled and chopped carrots
- 1 cup water
- 1 teaspoon maple syrup
- 1 small clove garlic, chopped
- 1 teaspoon extra-virgin olive oil
- ½ teaspoon firmly packed chopped fresh mint

Put all of the ingredients into a blender and process until almost smooth. Transfer to a medium-sized bowl. Cover and refrigerate 2 to 4 hours, or until well chilled. Stir before serving.

Super Chunky Soup

MAKES 10 SERVINGS

Big chunks of baby red potatoes, butternut squash and sweet potatoes make this simple to prepare potage a hearty offering for a weeknight meal. Thinly sliced Napa cabbage stands in for noodles while adding great taste.

- **11 cups water**
- **5 cups thinly sliced Napa cabbage**
- **4 cups peeled, seeded and cubed butternut squash**
- **4 cups cubed baby red potatoes**
- **4 cups peeled and cubed sweet potatoes**
- **3 cups cherry or grape tomatoes, sliced in half**
- **2 large vegan bouillon cubes, crumbled (see note)**
- **1 tablespoon finely chopped garlic**
- **1 tablespoon Italian seasoning blend**

Put all of the ingredients into a large soup pot. Cover and bring to a simmer over medium-high heat. Decrease the heat to medium-low and cook for 1 hour, stirring occasionally. Serve hot.

CHEF'S NOTE: If preferred, you may use 11 cups of prepared vegetable broth in place of the water and bouillon cubes.

Kale, Carrot and White Bean Soup

MAKES 4 TO 6 SERVINGS

When you want a warming soup in a hurry, this soup really fills the bill. Featuring fresh kale, carrots and other pantry ingredients, this recipe comes together in about 20 minutes. Perfect for easy fall fare or a mid-winter meal.

- 7 to 8 cups water, plus more as needed
- 3 large carrots, peeled and sliced
- 8 ounces cremini mushrooms, sliced
- 1 can (15 to 16 ounces) white beans, drained and rinsed
- 8 ounces fusilli pasta (or your favorite pasta variety)
- 1½ large vegan bouillon cubes
- 3 to 4 very large leaves of kale, stems removed and thinly sliced
- 1 teaspoon tamari
- Sea salt, to taste

Put the water, carrots, mushrooms, white beans, pasta and bouillon cubes into a large soup pot. Add more water if needed to cover the vegetables and pasta by about 2-inches.

Cover and bring to a boil over medium-high heat. Decrease the heat to medium-low and cook, stirring occasionally, for 12 minutes. Add the kale, cover and cook, stirring occasionally, for 3 minutes.

Stir in the tamari, cover and cook for 1 minute. Taste, and add salt if desired. Serve hot with crusty whole-grain bread on the side.

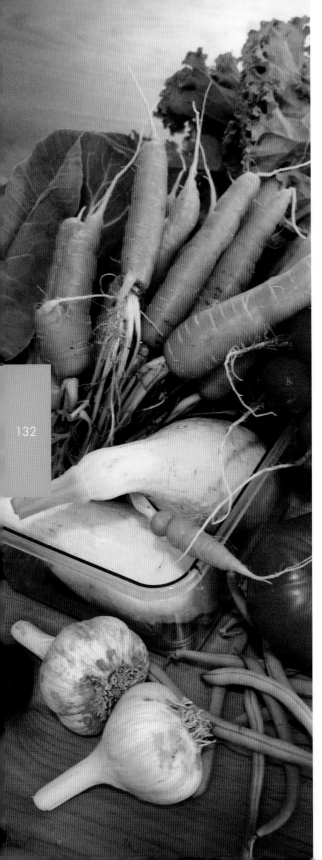

Farm Stand Soup

MAKES 8 SERVINGS

A visit to my local farm stand often results in a plethora of appetizing seasonal produce. After one such trip, I created this tasty and invigorating summer soup.

- 10 carrots, sliced (peeling is optional)
- 5 white potatoes, peeled and chopped
- 3 cloves garlic, minced
- 1 small bunch celery with leaves, sliced
- 1 medium yellow summer squash, seeded and cubed
- 1 red onion, chopped
- 2 teaspoons Italian seasoning blend
- 3 large vegan bouillon cubes, crumbled
- 10 cups water, plus more as needed
- 1½ cans (22 to 24 ounces) white beans, drained and rinsed
- 2 large collard leaves, thick stems removed and thinly sliced
- 2 to 3 large kale leaves, thick stems removed and thinly sliced
- 3 tablespoons chopped fresh parsley
- 10 basil leaves, thinly sliced, plus more for garnish (optional)

Put the carrots, potatoes, garlic, celery, squash, onion, Italian seasoning, bouillon and water into a large soup pot. Add more water as needed to cover the vegetables by about 1-inch. Cover and bring to a boil over medium-high heat. Decrease the heat to medium-low, cover and simmer, stirring occasionally, for 25 minutes.

Add the white beans, stir and add more water if needed. Cover and simmer, stirring occasionally, for 15 minutes. Add the collards, kale and parsley, cover and simmer, stirring occasionally, for about 15 minutes, or until the greens are wilted and the vegetables are tender. Stir in the basil and cook for 3 minutes more. Spoon into soup bowls and garnish with more basil, if desired. Serve piping hot.

Portobello Mushroom and Cabbage Soup

MAKES 8 SERVINGS

This satisfying soup makes an ideal weeknight meal. The portobello mushrooms add fantastic depth of flavor, while thinly sliced cabbage stands in for noodles. Low in calories, but high in nutrition *and* good taste!

- 3 cups peeled and diced yellow potatoes
- 3 cups peeled and diced sweet potatoes
- 2½ cups diced portobello mushrooms
- 2 cups sliced carrots (peeling is optional)
- 2 cups peeled and sliced parsnips
- 2 cloves garlic, minced
- ½ cup diced yellow or sweet onion
- 1 large vegan bouillon cube, crumbled
- 8 cups water, plus more as needed
- 6½ cups thinly sliced green cabbage
- 1 can (15 to 16 ounces) red kidney beans
- ¼ teaspoon sea salt, plus more to taste

Put the yellow potatoes, sweet potatoes, mushrooms, carrots, parsnips, garlic, onion, bouillon cube and water into a large soup pot. Add more water as needed to cover the vegetables by about 1-inch. Cover and bring to a simmer over medium-high heat. Decrease the heat to medium-low, cover and simmer for 25 minutes, stirring occasionally. Stir in the cabbage, cover and simmer for 20 to 25 minutes, stirring occasionally. Add the beans and sea salt. Cover and simmer for an additional 15 to 20 minutes, or until the veggies are soft and the kidney beans are heated through. Taste and add more salt, if desired. Serve piping hot with crusty bread or muffins on the side.

Thirty-Minute Veggie-Tofu Soup

MAKES 6 SERVINGS

My husband adores this soup and says it reminds him of a "Japanese-style" soup, but I love it because it's so tasty, nutritious *and* quick to prepare!

- 1 block (14 to 16 ounces) extra-firm regular tofu, drained
- 2 teaspoons tamari, divided
- 8 ounces cremini mushrooms, sliced
- 8 ounces whole-grain fusilli pasta
- 4 medium carrots, sliced (peeling is optional)
- 2 teaspoons extra-virgin olive oil
- ½ teaspoon all-purpose seasoning
- 1 large vegan bouillon cube, crumbled (see note)
- 10 to 12 cups water, plus more as needed
- 2 cups firmly packed baby spinach

Cut the tofu into ½-inch cubes and put it into a medium-sized bowl. Drizzle 1 teaspoon of the tamari over the tofu. Put the tofu in the refrigerator to marinate for 25 minutes.

Put the mushrooms, pasta, carrots, olive oil, seasoning and bouillon into a large soup pot. Pour the water over the top to cover the vegetables by about 1-inch. Cover and bring to a simmer over medium-high heat. Decrease the heat to medium-low, cover and cook, stirring occasionally, for 20 minutes.

Add the tofu and 1 teaspoon of tamari. Cover and cook for 7 minutes, stirring occasionally. Add the spinach and cook for 3 minutes. Serve hot.

CHEF'S NOTE: You may use prepared vegetable broth in place of the bouillon cube and water, if desired.

Tricolore Orzo Soup

MAKES 4 SERVINGS

This lively soup makes a great first course or light lunch. Orzo is a rice-shaped pasta that resembles rice, but cooks up quickly in this easy potage.

- 4 cups vegetable broth
- ½ cup water
- 1 large carrot, diced
- 1 scallion, white and green parts, sliced
- 1 tablespoon chopped fresh flat-leaf parsley, plus more for garnish
- 1 teaspoon tamari
- ¾ cup *tricolore* orzo
- Sea salt, to taste
- Freshly ground pepper, to taste
- Several sprigs chopped fresh parsley, to garnish

Put the broth and water in a medium-sized saucepan over medium-high heat and bring to a boil. Stir in the carrot, scallion, parsley and tamari. Decrease the heat to medium-low, cover and simmer for about 8 minutes. Stir in the orzo and simmer, stirring occasionally, until the orzo and carrots are tender, about 10 minutes. Season with salt and pepper to taste. To serve, ladle the soup into bowls. Garnish with parsley, if desired.

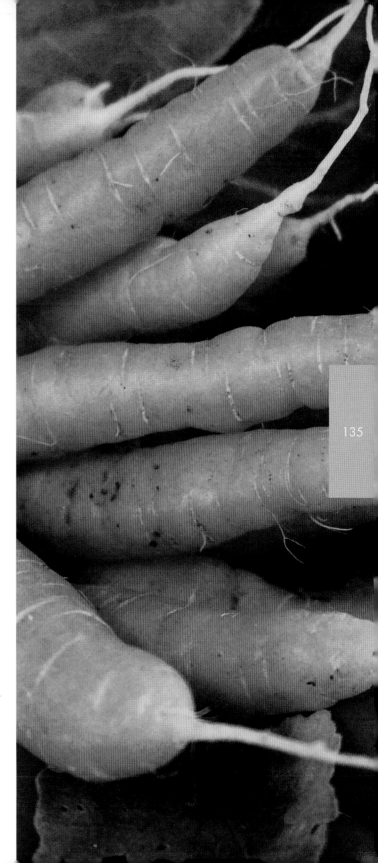

Fresh and Easy Potato-Vegetable Soup

MAKES 8 SERVINGS

On the weekends, I like to make a big pot of soup that will last into the week. This delightfully easy, quick and delicious combo, featuring common root veggies, makes a hearty offering.

- 2 pounds Yukon Gold potatoes, peeled and cubed
- 2 large sweet potatoes or yams, peeled and cubed
- 5 medium carrots, sliced (peeling is optional)
- 5 stalks celery, with leaves, sliced
- 10 ounces white button or cremini mushrooms, sliced
- 4 to 5 cloves of garlic, minced
- 1 tablespoon Italian seasoning blend
- 2 large vegan bouillon cubes, crumbled
- 2 teaspoons extra-virgin olive oil
- 8 to 10 cups water, plus more as needed
- 12 ounces cooked *tricolore* radiatore or fusilli pasta

Put the Yukon Gold potatoes, sweet potatoes, carrots, celery, mushrooms, garlic, Italian seasoning blend, bouillon cubes and olive oil into a large soup pot. Add water to cover the vegetables by about 1-inch. Cover and bring to a simmer over medium-high heat. Decrease the heat to medium-low and simmer, stirring occasionally, for 50 minutes to 1 hour.

Meanwhile, bring a large pot of salted water to boil over medium-high heat. Stir in the pasta. Decrease the heat to medium-low and cook, stirring occasionally, until the pasta is cooked *al dente*.

To serve, put one-eighth of the pasta into the bottom of a soup bowl. Top with a generous serving of the soup, and serve.

Roasted Carrot and Butternut Squash Soup with Cinnamon-Maple "Cream"

MAKES 4 TO 5 SERVINGS

This enticing soup provides an elegant start to a fancy meal, or pairs nicely with a sandwich for a filling supper.

SOUP

- 3½ cups peeled, seeded and cubed butternut squash (cut in about ½-inch cubes)
- 2 cups sliced carrots (peeling is optional)
- 2 teaspoons extra-virgin olive oil
- 2 teaspoons Italian seasoning blend
- ¼ teaspoon sea salt, divided, plus more to taste
- 2 cups unsweetened nondairy milk
- 1 cup water, plus more as needed
- 1 tablespoon maple syrup
- ⅛ teaspoon ground cinnamon
- basil leaves or parsley sprigs (for garnish)

....

CINNAMON-MAPLE "CREAM" (see note)

- ½ block (7 to 8 ounces) firm regular tofu, drained
- 1 tablespoon maple syrup
- ⅛ teaspoon ground cinnamon

Preheat the oven to 375 degrees F. Line a large, rimmed baking sheet with unbleached parchment paper.

Put the squash, carrots, olive oil, Italian seasoning and ⅛ teaspoon sea salt into a large bowl and toss gently until the vegetables are thoroughly coated with the oil, seasoning and salt. Arrange the squash and carrot mixture in a single layer on the lined pan. Bake for 50 to 60 minutes, stirring once or twice, until the squash and carrots are quite soft and slightly golden. Put the pan on a wire rack and let the carrots and squash cool for 20 minutes (see note).

While the squash and carrots cool, make the "cream." Put the tofu, 1 tablespoon maple syrup and ⅛ teaspoon ground cinnamon into a blender and process until smooth and creamy. Transfer to a small bowl, cover and refrigerate until serving.

To make the soup, put the cooled squash and carrots, nondairy milk, water, 1 tablespoon maple syrup, ⅛ teaspoon sea salt and ⅛ teaspoon ground cinnamon into a blender and process until smooth, adding more water, about ¼ cup at a time, to achieve the desired consistency.

Pour the soup into a medium-sized saucepan, cover and cook over medium-low heat for 10 to 12 minutes, stirring often, until heated through. Season with more sea salt, to taste.

To serve, ladle the soup into small soup bowls. Using a spoon, swirl about 1 tablespoon of the Cinnamon-Maple "Cream" (see note) into the top of each serving in a pleasing pattern, garnish with a basil leaf or fresh parsley, and serve.

CHEF'S NOTES:

· The squash and carrots may be roasted up to 24 hours ahead of time. After cooling, transfer to an airtight container and refrigerate until use.

· The recipe for Cinnamon-Maple "Cream" will make more than needed for this recipe. Stored tightly covered in the refrigerator, it will keep for 2 days and is delicious served with a fruit crisp, pie, cake, pancakes or spooned over granola.

· After the soup is blended it may be cooled thoroughly, packed in a tightly sealed container and stored in the refrigerator for up to 24 hours. To serve, pour into a medium-sized saucepan, cover and simmer over medium-low heat for about 20 minutes, stirring often, until heated through. The soup will thicken in the refrigerator, so before re-heating, add more nondairy milk or water to achieve the desired consistency.

Carrot, Split Pea and Potato Soup

MAKES 6 SERVINGS

- 1 pound dried split peas, sorted and rinsed
- 3 cups peeled and cubed white or Yukon Gold potatoes
- 2½ cups sliced carrots (peeling is optional)
- 7 cups water, plus more as needed
- 1 tablespoon extra-virgin olive oil
- 2 teaspoons tamari
- ½ teaspoon dried rubbed sage
- ½ teaspoon dried crushed rosemary
- ½ teaspoon dried thyme
- ½ teaspoon garlic powder
- ⅛ teaspoon cayenne pepper
- Sea salt, to taste (optional)

So hearty, this soup makes the perfect one-pot meal on a cold day. Delicately flavored with a few key ingredients, it is surprisingly filling and tasty. Bonus: it's extremely economical too.

Put the ingredients into a large soup pot. Add more water, if needed, to cover the peas and carrots by about 1-inch. Cover and bring to a simmer over medium heat. Decrease the heat to medium-low, cover and simmer for 60 to 80 minutes, stirring occasionally, or until the peas are soft. Add more water, as needed, if the soup becomes too thick. If desired, mash the soup gently with a potato masher to break up the potatoes slightly. Season with salt, to taste. Serve hot.

CHEF'S NOTE: Put any leftover soup into a tightly covered container and refrigerate for up to 3 days. The soup will thicken considerably as it chills. Before reheating, stir the soup well and add more water as needed to thin the soup to the desired consistency.

Sweet Potato and Cauliflower Bisque

MAKES 2 TO 4 SERVINGS

This bisque-style soup highlights the creamy texture of sweet potatoes, red potatoes and cauliflower. It is a dream to prepare, as it has few ingredients and needs little prep time. This hearty potage makes a nice light lunch or a delicious first course option.

- ¼ of a large head of cauliflower, coarsely chopped
- 2 medium red potatoes, peeled and cubed
- 1 medium sweet potato, peeled and cubed
- 1 cup vegetable broth, plus more as needed
- 1 cup unsweetened nondairy milk
- ¼ teaspoon sea salt, plus more as needed
- ¼ teaspoon tamari

Fit a steamer basket into a medium-sized saucepan with a tight-fitting lid. Add 2 inches of cold water, then add the cauliflower, red potatoes and sweet potatoes. Cover and bring to a boil. Steam the vegetables for about 20 minutes, until tender. Transfer to a large bowl and let cool for 20 minutes.

Put the cauliflower, red potatoes, sweet potatoes, vegetable broth, nondairy milk, salt and tamari into a blender and process until smooth. Add more broth, ¼ cup at a time, as needed to achieve the desired consistency.

Pour into a medium-sized saucepan, cover and cook over medium-low heat for 10 to 12 minutes, stirring frequently, until heated through. Serve piping hot.

CHEF'S NOTE: After the soup is blended it may be cooled thoroughly, packed in a tightly sealed container and stored in the refrigerator for up to 24 hours. To serve, pour into a medium-sized saucepan, cover and simmer over medium-low heat for about 20 minutes, stirring often, until heated through. The soup will thicken in the refrigerator, so before re-heating, add more broth or nondairy milk to achieve the desired consistency.

Cauliflower-Leek Soup with Sweet Paprika

MAKES 3 TO 4 SERVINGS

This creamy soup gets a kick from sweet paprika and a touch of brown sugar for the perfect balance of flavors.

- 1 small head of cauliflower, chopped
- 2½ cups thinly sliced leeks (include light green parts), cleaned well
- 1½ cups vegetable broth, plus more as needed
- 2 heaping teaspoons dark brown sugar
- ½ teaspoon sweet paprika, plus more for garnish
- ½ teaspoon Italian seasoning blend
- ½ teaspoon extra-virgin olive oil
- ¼ teaspoon sea salt

Fit a steamer basket into a medium-sized saucepan with a tight-fitting lid. Add 2 inches of cold water, and then add the cauliflower and leeks. Cover and bring to a boil. Steam the cauliflower and leeks for about 12 to 15 minutes, until tender. Transfer to a large bowl and let cool for 20 minutes.

Put the cauliflower and leeks, vegetable broth, brown sugar, paprika, Italian seasoning, olive oil and salt into a blender and process until smooth. Add more broth, ¼ cup at a time, as needed to achieve the desired consistency.

Pour into a medium-sized saucepan, cover and cook over medium-low heat for 10 to 12 minutes, stirring frequently, until heated through. Ladle into soup bowls and garnish with more sweet paprika, if desired. Serve piping hot.

CHEF'S NOTE: After the soup is blended it may be cooled thoroughly, packed in a tightly sealed container and stored in the refrigerator for up to 24 hours. To serve, pour into a medium-sized saucepan, cover and simmer over medium-low heat for about 20 minutes, stirring often, until heated through. The soup will thicken in the refrigerator, so before re-heating, add more broth to achieve the desired consistency.

CHAPTER NINE
Lunch, Brunch or Light Supper

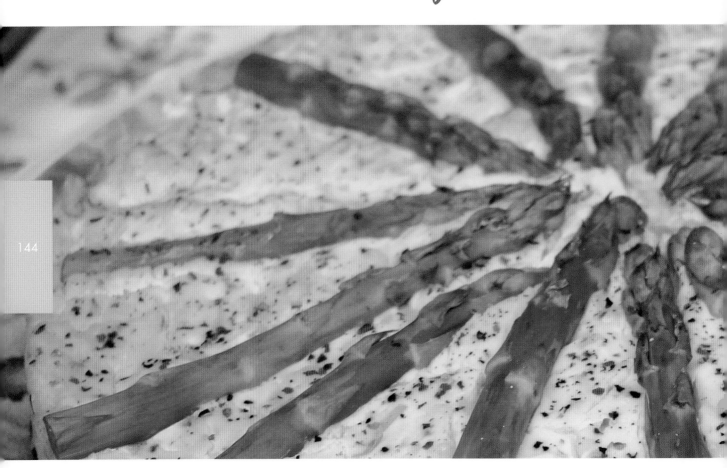

Call it lunch, or call it brunch—a mid-day meal is always a favorite of mine! Whether it's a tasty sandwich, fancy quiche or one-dish bowl, delicious and nutritious late morning or early afternoon fare can keep you going strong until supper.

Recipes

Asparagus Tart

MAKES 8 SERVINGS

This amazing dish is a tasty cross between a veggie quiche and a crustless tart. It's simple to prepare, pretty to serve and *delicious* to eat!

- 1 block (14 to 16 ounces) extra-firm regular tofu, drained
- 1 aseptic box (12 to 12½ ounces) extra-firm silken tofu, drained
- 1 tablespoon unsweetened nondairy milk
- ½ teaspoon sea salt
- ½ teaspoon ground turmeric
- ½ teaspoon garlic powder
- ⅛ teaspoon freshly ground black pepper, plus more to taste
- ½ cup shredded vegan cheddar-style cheese
- 2 teaspoons Italian seasoning blend
- 1 medium sweet onion, finely diced
- 14 asparagus stalks, cut into 4 to 4½-inch lengths

Preheat the oven to 350 degrees F. Generously coat a 9-inch round springform pan with vegan margarine.

Put the regular tofu, silken tofu, nondairy milk, salt, turmeric, garlic powder and pepper into a blender or food processor and process until smooth.

Fold in the vegan cheddar cheese, Italian seasoning and onion, using a rubber spatula. Transfer the tofu mixture to the prepared pan and smooth the top with the back of a rubber spatula. Arrange the 14 asparagus spears over the top of the tart to resemble the spokes of a wheel (trimming them to fit as you go), with the asparagus tips forming the center of the "wheel."

Top the tart with several grinds of black pepper. Bake for 45 to 55 minutes, or until the center of the tart is quite firm to the touch. Put the pan on a wire rack and let cool 5 minutes.

Gently run a table knife around the perimeter of the tart to loosen it from the sides of the pan. Let cool for 5 to 7 minutes, then carefully remove the outer ring of the springform pan.

Let the tart cool for 30 minutes more before serving (see note). Alternately, cover the tart and refrigerate for 4 to 6 hours, or until well chilled, and serve cold.

CHEF'S NOTE: When served warm, the tart will be quite soft, so slice it carefully for serving. The tart will firm up quite a bit after it is refrigerated for 4 to 6 hours.

Zucchini Quiche Cups with Rustic Bread Crusts

MAKES 6 SERVINGS

- 3 very large slices whole-grain, country style bread (see note)
- ½ block (7 to 8 ounces) extra-firm regular tofu, drained
- 1 tablespoon water
- 2 teaspoons Dijon mustard
- 2 teaspoons extra-virgin olive oil, plus more for brushing
- 1 teaspoon reduced-sodium tamari
- ¼ teaspoon ground turmeric
- 1 cup shredded zucchini, plus 6 thin slices
- ½ cup shredded vegan cheese
- Freshly ground black pepper, to taste
- Dash chili powder

These little quiche cups will wake up any meal of the day, but they are especially appetizing for a casual late-morning or mid-day brunch meal. A crispy little bread crust cradles a deliciously smooth and creamy tofu and zucchini filling.

Preheat the oven to 375 degrees F. Thoroughly coat a 6-cup jumbo muffin tin with vegan margarine.

Put 1 slice of bread on a cutting board. Compress the bread slice to ⅛-to ¼-inch thick, using a rolling pin. Cut the bread into two triangles (see note). Prepare the remaining 2 bread slices in the same manner. Gently press each bread triangle into a muffin cup to form a rustic crust (the bread does not have to fit perfectly into the cup).

Put the tofu, water, Dijon mustard, olive oil, tamari and turmeric into a high-performance blending appliance and process until very smooth. Fold in 1 cup shredded zucchini and the vegan cheese, using a rubber spatula.

Evenly divide the filling into each of the 6 prepared muffin cups. Put a zucchini slice in the center of each quiche cup. Smooth the top and brush each quiche cup with a bit of olive oil. Sprinkle each quiche cup with several grinds of black pepper and a dash of chili powder. Cover loosely with parchment paper and bake for 30 minutes. Uncover and bake for an additional 5 to 10 minutes, or until slightly golden. The centers of the quiche will be slightly soft. Transfer the pan to a wire rack and loosen the sides of each quiche cup with a knife. Let rest for 10 minutes, and then carefully lift each quiche cup out of the pan. Serve warm, or refrigerate for 3 to 6 hours and serve cold.

CHEF'S NOTE: If you do not have large slices of bread, use 6 smaller slices of bread. If you are using smaller slices of bread, after you roll the bread out, do not cut it into two triangles. Proceed with recipe as directed.

Spinach, Onion and Red Pepper Crustless Quiche

MAKES 6 SERVINGS

Creating a dairy free, egg free *and* gluten-free quiche recipe can be challenging, but this flavorful version is so yummy you won't miss the dairy, eggs or crust!

- 1 block (14 to 16 ounces) extra-firm regular tofu, drained
- 3 tablespoons unsweetened nondairy milk
- 2 teaspoons reduced-sodium tamari
- 2 teaspoons extra-virgin olive oil
- 1 teaspoon ground turmeric
- ¼ teaspoon smoked paprika
- 1½ cups diced sweet onion
- 1 cup seeded and sliced sweet mini peppers
- ¾ cup shredded vegan cheese
- ¼ cup minced fresh flat leaf parsley
- 4 cups lightly packed baby spinach
- ¼ scant teaspoon sweet paprika

Preheat the oven to 350 degrees F. Generously coat a 10-inch round quiche dish with vegan margarine. Put the tofu, nondairy milk, tamari, olive oil, turmeric and smoked paprika into a blender and process for about 30 seconds, until smooth. Transfer the mixture to a large mixing bowl.

Add the onion, peppers, vegan cheese and parsley, and gently stir to combine. Fold in the baby spinach. Transfer the mixture to the prepared dish. Sprinkle the top with the sweet paprika.

Bake for 25 to 35 minutes, or until the quiche is set and starts to crack (see note). Put the pan on a wire rack and gently loosen the sides of the quiche, using a kitchen knife. Let cool for 20 to 30 minutes before carefully slicing (quiche will still be somewhat soft). Serve warm (see note) with a crisp salad on the side. Cover the leftover quiche and store in the refrigerator for up to 2 days.

CHEF'S NOTES:

- Depending upon the type of vegan cheese that you use, you may need to bake the quiche for up to 40 minutes.
- This quiche is *delicious* served chilled! After the quiche has cooled, cover and refrigerate for 4 to 6 hours, and serve cold.

Chickpea-Avocado Sandwich Wrap

MAKES 3 SERVINGS

So satisfying, this sandwich wrap takes the place of an egg or chicken salad sandwich. Excellent for packing into a lunchbox or for serving at a ladies luncheon, this delightful combination of flavors and textures is sure to please.

- 3 whole-grain sandwich wraps
- 1 recipe *Carrot-Chickpea Sandwich Spread* (page 155)
- 1 medium avocado, peeled, pitted and sliced
- 3 handfuls baby spring lettuce mix

Put a sandwich wrap on a dinner plate.

Spread one-third of the *Carrot-Chickpea Sandwich Spread*, a few avocado slices and a handful of baby greens in the center of the sandwich wrap. Roll the wrap up very tightly, folding the sides in as you go, ending with the seam side down. Slice diagonally into 2 pieces. Repeat with the other 2 wraps, and serve.

Avocado-Salsa Sandwich (See photo on page 11.)

MAKES 2 SERVINGS

Let's dance the salsa! This quick, nutritious sandwich makes an easy luncheon entrée or a great morning meal.

- 4 slices whole-grain or country-style bread
- 1 large avocado, peeled, pitted and sliced
- 10 to 12 cherry or grape tomatoes, sliced in half
- 6 teaspoons prepared salsa, plus more as needed

Put 2 slices of bread on each of two plates. Arrange one-quarter of the avocado slices, one-quarter of the tomato halves and one-quarter of the prepared salsa over each slice of bread, and serve.

French Lentil Salad Bowl with Sweet Peppers and Basil

MAKES 4 SERVINGS

Lentils provide a substantial base and plenty of plant-based protein, while the veggies and flavorings add zing to this satisfying salad.

- 4 cups cooked French green lentils, well chilled (see note)
- ⅔ cup diced sweet onion
- 1 medium red sweet bell pepper, seeded and chopped
- 1 large avocado, peeled, pitted and chopped
- ½ cup chopped fresh basil
- 2 tablespoons extra-virgin olive oil
- 2 tablespoons freshly squeezed lemon juice
- 1 heaping teaspoon chili powder
- ½ teaspoon sea salt

Put all of the ingredients into a large bowl and gently stir to combine. Spoon into deep bowls and serve at room temperature, or cover and refrigerate for up to 2 hours and serve cold.

CHEF'S NOTE: Lentils don't need to be presoaked, but make sure to check for small stones before preparing, and be certain to rinse them well. To cook the lentils, put 4 cups water with 2 cups lentils into a large saucepan and bring to a boil over medium-high heat. Decrease the heat to low, cover and cook for 35 to 40 minutes, stirring occasionally. Add more water if the pan becomes dry. The lentils are done when they are soft (they do not need to absorb all of the water). Drain off any excess water in a fine meshed strainer. Yields 4 to 5 cups cooked lentils.

SALAD

- 3 cups cooked and cooled quinoa (page 237, see variation)
- 2½ cups seeded and diced sweet bell peppers (combination of red, orange and yellow)
- 1 cup pitted and chopped Kalamata olives
- 1 medium cucumber, thinly sliced
- 1 can (15 to 16 ounces) chickpeas (garbanzo beans) drained and rinsed
- 1 large clove garlic, minced

DRESSING

- 2½ tablespoons freshly squeezed lemon juice
- 1¼ tablespoons freshly squeezed lime juice
- 2 tablespoons extra-virgin olive oil
- 1 teaspoon all-purpose seasoning
- ¼ teaspoon ground turmeric
- ⅛ teaspoon cayenne pepper
- Sea salt, to taste
- Freshly ground pepper, to taste

GARNISHES (optional)

- Avocado slices
- Fresh chopped parsley
- Smoked tofu

Quinoa Luncheon Bowl with Lemon-Lime Dressing

MAKES 4 TO 6 SERVINGS

I love to make a hearty quinoa salad during the warm weather months. It's colorful to serve and filling to eat—perfect for a simple luncheon entrée or light summer supper.

Put the salad ingredients into a large bowl and gently toss to combine. Put all of the dressing ingredients into a small bowl and briskly whisk until smooth and emulsified.

Pour the dressing over the salad and gently stir, to coat. Taste and add salt and pepper, if desired. Serve at once, or cover and refrigerate for 2 to 4 hours and serve chilled. To serve, spoon into individual bowls and top with optional garnishes, if desired.

Carrot-Chickpea Spread in *Tortilla Bowls*

Carrot-Chickpea Sandwich Spread

MAKES 3 TO 4 SERVINGS

If you're craving a terrific plant-based substitute for egg salad or chicken salad, search no further. The texture, taste and delicate flavors of this sandwich spread are both satisfying and hearty. It also makes a tasty appetizer spread served with flatbread or crackers, or scooped into *Cute Little Tortilla Bowls* (page 156).

- 1 can (15 to 16 ounces) chickpeas (garbanzo beans), drained and rinsed

- 2 tablespoons vegan mayonnaise, plus more as needed

- 1 tablespoon Dijon mustard

- ¼ teaspoon chili powder

- ¼ teaspoon smoked paprika

- ¼ teaspoon sea salt, plus more as needed

- Several grinds of freshly ground black pepper, plus more as needed

- ⅔ cup grated carrots (peeling is optional)

- 1 tablespoon capers, drained and rinsed

Put the chickpeas, mayonnaise, Dijon mustard, chili powder and paprika into a medium-sized bowl and mash using a potato masher or large fork until combined, but still chunky. Taste and add more vegan mayonnaise, if desired. Add the sea salt and freshly ground pepper, and stir to combine.

Fold in the grated carrots and capers. Season with more salt or pepper, to taste. Serve at room temperature, or cover and refrigerate for 2 to 4 hours, and serve cold.

VARIATION: Carrot-Chickpea Spread in Tortilla Bowls – (Makes 10 to 12 servings) For a festive appetizer-style presentation, line the bottom of 10 to 12 *Cute Little Tortilla Bowls* (page 156) with finely chopped Napa cabbage or romaine lettuce. Top with a small scoop of the *Carrot-Chickpea Spread* and garnish with tiny carrot sticks and mini-red pepper slices. Arrange the little bowls on a pretty platter and serve.

Cute Little Tortilla Bowls

MAKES 12 BOWLS

These edible bowls make an enticing base for *Curried "No-Chicken" Spread* (opposite page), *Carrot-Chickpea-Sandwich Spread* (page 155), *Smoky and Spicy Guacamole* (page 56) or any tasty filling you prefer. These dainty bowls are wonderful as part of a buffet table, appetizer course or outdoor picnic. So quick to make, too!

• **3 whole wheat or whole-grain tortillas (each 10 to 11-inches in diameter) (see note)**

Preheat the oven to 350 degrees F. Put a tortilla on a cutting board and cut out 4 rounds using a 4 to 4½-inch round cookie cutter. Repeat with the remaining tortillas, making 12 tortilla rounds in all.

Carefully press a tortilla round inside each cup of a 12-cup jumbo muffin tin (or two 6-cup jumbo muffin tins). Repeat with the remaining tortilla rounds, so that each jumbo cup is snugly lined with a tortilla round, making 12 cups in all.

Bake for 6 to 9 minutes, or until the tortilla bowls are almost firm and slightly golden on the bottom and around the edges. Transfer the tortilla bowls to a wire rack and let cool for at least 20 minutes before filling and serving. Stored in a tightly covered container in the refrigerator, tortilla bowls will keep up to 4 days.

CHEF'S NOTE: For a gluten-free option, use your favorite gluten-free tortilla, such as a brown rice tortilla.

Curried "No-Chicken" Spread

MAKES 2 TO 3 SERVINGS

A bit of spice makes this enticing spread very nice. Serve it in pita pockets or between two thick slices of whole-grain bread.

- 1 can (15 to 16 ounces) chickpeas, (garbanzo beans) drained and rinsed

- 2 tablespoons sesame tahini, plus more as needed

- 1 tablespoon water, plus more as needed

- 3 stalks celery with leaves, diced

- 1 teaspoon ground cumin

- ½ teaspoon ground turmeric

- ½ teaspoon all-purpose seasoning

- ¼ teaspoon sea salt, plus more as needed

Put the chickpeas, tahini and water into a medium-sized bowl and mash well using a potato masher or large fork. Add all of the other ingredients, and stir with a large spoon to combine. Taste, and add more salt, tahini or a bit more water, as desired. Serve at room temperature, or cover and refrigerate for 2 hours, and serve cold.

CHAPTER TEN
Pasta Love

I love pasta in all shapes and sizes! Pasta makes a fabulous main event, side dish or foundation for a hearty casserole. From festive fusilli to lovely lasagna, pasta is a favorite in the *Jazzy Vegetarian* kitchen!

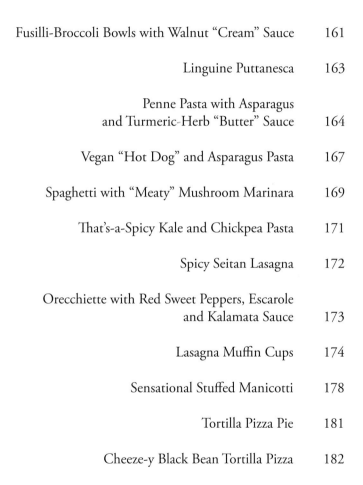

Recipes

Fusilli-Broccoli Bowls with Walnut "Cream" Sauce

MAKES 2 TO 3 SERVINGS

Easy to double, this creamy tasting pasta dish comes together in about 20 minutes and makes an enticing family weeknight meal or a casual party dish.

- •8 ounces fusilli pasta
- •4 cups bite-sized broccoli florets
- •1 to 1½ cups *Walnut "Cream" Sauce,* plus more as needed (page 70)
- •Sea salt, to taste
- •1 tablespoon roasted or raw sunflower seeds (optional), for garnish
- •Fresh chopped parsley (optional), for garnish

Bring a large pot of salted water to boil over medium-high heat. Stir in the fusilli. Decrease the heat to medium-low and cook, stirring occasionally, for 8 minutes. Add the broccoli florets, stir and cook for 3 to 4 minutes, or until the fusilli and broccoli are both cooked *al dente.*

Drain the fusilli and broccoli. Transfer the fusilli/broccoli mixture to a large bowl, and stir in 1 cup of the Walnut "Cream" Sauce. Gently combine, adding more walnut sauce, as needed, to thoroughly coat the fusilli. Season with sea salt, to taste. Garnish with optional sunflower seeds and parsley, if desired. Spoon into pasta bowls and serve immediately.

Linguine Puttanesca

MAKES 4 SERVINGS

A mix of celery, beans, capers and diverse seasonings are showcased in this spicy pasta sauce. There are quite a few ingredients, but few cooking steps, so this is an ideal dish to serve for a substantial weeknight meal.

- 2½ cups chopped celery, with leaves
- 1 medium sweet onion, chopped
- 1 cup water, plus more as needed
- 2 teaspoons extra-virgin olive oil
- 1 teaspoon reduced-sodium tamari
- 1 teaspoon dried oregano
- 1 teaspoon dried marjoram
- ½ teaspoon dried thyme
- ¼ teaspoon crushed dried rosemary
- ¼ teaspoon crushed red pepper
- 1 jar (24 to 26 ounces) vegan marinara sauce
- 1 can (15 to 20 ounces) cannellini beans, drained and rinsed
- 3 tablespoons capers, drained and rinsed
- 1 pound whole-grain linguine, fettuccine or spaghetti

Put the celery, onion, ⅓ cup water, olive oil, tamari, oregano, marjoram, thyme, rosemary and crushed pepper into a large skillet. Cover and bring to a simmer over medium heat. Decrease the heat to medium-low, cover and simmer for 10 to 15 minutes, stirring occasionally, until the celery and onions are soft. Add more water, 2 tablespoons at a time as needed, to keep the celery and onions from sticking to the bottom of the pan.

Stir in the marinara sauce and ⅓ cup water. Cover and cook for 30 minutes, stirring occasionally.

Stir in the beans, capers and remaining ⅓ cup water. Cover and simmer for 20 to 25 minutes, or until the sauce has cooked down and thickened.

Meanwhile, bring a large pot of salted water to a boil over medium-high heat. Stir in the linguine. Decrease the heat to medium-low and cook, stirring occasionally, until the linguine is cooked *al dente*. Drain the linguine.

Divide the linguine evenly between four pasta bowls and top with a liberal serving of sauce. Serve immediately.

Penne Pasta with Asparagus and Turmeric-Herb "Butter" Sauce

MAKES 4 SERVINGS

So simple but oh-so-satisfying, this one-pot pasta makes great use of fresh spring asparagus. The entire dish whips up in less than 20 minutes, making this an ideal solution for a delicious, home-cooked weeknight meal.

- 1 pound penne pasta
- 4½ cups fresh asparagus, trimmed and cut in 1½ to 2-inch lengths
- 3 tablespoons vegan margarine, plus more as needed
- 1 teaspoon dried parsley, or 1 tablespoon chopped fresh parsley
- 1 teaspoon dried basil, or 1 tablespoon chopped fresh basil
- ¼ teaspoon dried marjoram
- ¼ teaspoon garlic powder
- ¼ teaspoon sea salt, plus more as needed
- ⅛ teaspoon ground turmeric
- Freshly ground black pepper, to taste

Bring a large pot of salted water to a boil over medium-high heat. Stir in the penne. Decrease the heat to medium-low and cook, stirring occasionally, for 8 minutes. Add the asparagus, stir and cook for 3 to 4 minutes, or until the penne is *al dente*, and the asparagus is crisp tender.

Meanwhile put the margarine, parsley, basil, marjoram, garlic powder, sea salt and turmeric into a bowl large enough to also accommodate the penne and the asparagus, and whip vigorously with a fork, until well combined.

Drain the penne and asparagus, and while they are still piping hot, pour them over the margarine mixture. Toss gently until thoroughly combined. Season with more salt and freshly ground pepper, to taste, and toss again. If the pasta seems slightly dry, add a bit more vegan margarine, to taste. Serve immediately.

Vegan "Hot Dog" and Asparagus Pasta

MAKES 4 TO 5 SERVINGS

This kid-pleasing pasta dish really saves the day when everyone craves the traditional taste of old-fashioned hot dogs but without the meat! Asparagus adds freshness and nutrition, while the *tricolore* pasta provides a pretty color. Give it a try—you and your family are going to love it.

- 1 pound fresh asparagus, trimmed and cut into bite-sized pieces (see note)
- 20 grape tomatoes
- 1 tablespoon plus 1 teaspoon extra-virgin olive oil, divided, plus more as needed
- ½ teaspoon garlic powder
- ¼ teaspoon chili powder
- ⅛ teaspoon cayenne pepper (optional)
- 4 vegan hotdogs, sliced
- 12 ounces *tricolore* fusilli (or your preferred pasta variety)
- ½ teaspoon reduced-sodium tamari, plus more to taste
- Sea salt, to taste
- Freshly ground black pepper, to taste

Preheat the oven to 400 degrees F. Line a large, rimmed baking sheet with unbleached parchment paper.

Put the asparagus, grape tomatoes, 1 tablespoon olive oil, garlic powder, chili powder and optional cayenne pepper into a large bowl. Toss to coat. Gently stir in the vegan hot dog slices.

Arrange the asparagus/vegan hot dog mixture in an even layer on the prepared baking sheet. Bake for 9 to 12 minutes or until the asparagus is tender and vegan hot dogs are heated through.

Meanwhile, bring a large pot of salted water to a boil over medium-high heat. Stir in the fusilli. Decrease the heat to medium-low and cook, stirring occasionally, until *al dente*. Drain the fusilli.

Transfer the drained fusilli to a large bowl. Immediately toss with 1 teaspoon olive oil and ½ teaspoon tamari. Season with salt and pepper, to taste. Taste and add more olive oil and/or tamari, to taste. Add the roasted asparagus/vegan hotdog mixture and gently toss to combine. Serve immediately.

CHEF'S NOTE: If preferred, you may substitute 1 medium head of broccoli cut into bite-sized florets, in place of the asparagus. Proceed with recipe as directed.

Spaghetti with "Meaty" Mushroom Marinara

MAKES 4 TO 6 SERVINGS

This tangy and sweet marinara sauce is a breeze to prepare, but it's packed with full-bodied flavor, enhanced by the pleasing taste and texture of mushrooms.

- 1 medium sweet onion, diced

- 1 tablespoon Italian seasoning blend

- 1 tablespoon extra-virgin olive oil

- 2 teaspoons reduced-sodium tamari

- ¼ teaspoon crushed red pepper

- ¼ cup water, plus more as needed

- 14 to 16 ounces white button or cremini mushrooms, sliced

- 1 can (26 to 28 ounces) whole fire-roasted tomatoes, with juice, lightly mashed

- 2 teaspoons maple syrup

- 1 pound spaghetti (or your favorite pasta variety)

Put the onion, Italian seasoning, olive oil, tamari and crushed red pepper into a large sauté pan and stir to combine, using a large spoon. Pour ¼ cup water over the onion mixture. Cover and cook over medium heat, for 6 to 7 minutes, stirring occasionally, or until the onion begins to become transparent. Decrease the heat to medium-low, and add the mushrooms.

Cook uncovered for 7 to 10 minutes, stirring occasionally, adding a bit more water as needed if the pan becomes dry. Stir in the tomatoes and maple syrup. Cover and cook for 45 to 50 minutes, stirring occasionally.

While the sauce cooks, bring a large pot of salted water to a boil over medium-high heat. Stir in the spaghetti. Decrease the heat to medium-low and cook, stirring occasionally, until *al dente*. Drain the spaghetti.

Divide the spaghetti into pasta bowls and top with a generous serving of the sauce. Serve immediately.

That's-a-Spicy Kale and Chickpea Pasta

MAKES 4 SERVINGS

This zesty and colorful pasta dish showcases two of my favorite foods... chickpeas and kale! Lightly sautéed in a light, but robustly flavored broth, then spooned over *tricolore* pasta, this enticing dish makes a satisfying weeknight meal.

- 1 large sweet onion, thinly sliced

- 1 tablespoon extra-virgin olive oil

- ½ cup plus 3 tablespoons water, divided, plus more as needed

- 1 teaspoon Italian seasoning blend

- ½ heaping teaspoon smoked paprika

- 12 ounces *tricolore* fusilli (or your favorite pasta variety)

- 1 small bunch dinosaur (lacinato) kale, thick stems removed, and chopped

- 1 can (15 to 16 ounces) chickpeas (garbanzo beans), drained and rinsed

- ½ large vegan bouillon cube, crumbled

- ½ teaspoon crushed red pepper

Put the onion, olive oil, 3 tablespoons water, Italian seasoning and smoked paprika into a large sauté pan. Cover and cook over medium heat for 10 minutes, stirring occasionally, adding more water if the pan becomes dry.

Meanwhile, bring a large pot of salted water to a boil over medium-high heat. Stir in the fusilli. Decrease the heat to medium-low and cook, stirring occasionally, until just *al dente*. Drain the fusilli.

While the fusilli cooks, stir the kale, chickpeas, bouillon and crushed red pepper into the onion mixture. Add the remaining ½ cup water. Decrease the heat to medium-low, cover and cook, stirring occasionally, for 7 to 10 minutes, or until the kale is wilted and the chickpeas are cooked through.

Add the fusilli to the sauce and gently stir to combine. Let cook 30 seconds to 1 minute. Serve immediately.

This protein packed, filling lasagna assembles for the oven in about 30 minutes or so, making it ideal for a weeknight meal. Need a gluten-free option? Simply use gluten-free lasagna noodles and swap out sautéed mushrooms for the seitan.

Spicy Seitan Lasagna

MAKES 6 SERVINGS

SPICY TOFU RICOTTA

- 1 block (14 to 16 ounces) extra-firm regular tofu, drained
- ½ medium lemon, freshly squeezed
- 2 teaspoons Italian seasoning blend
- 1 teaspoon garlic powder
- ¼ teaspoon cayenne pepper
- ¼ teaspoon sea salt

LASAGNA

- 12 whole-grain or whole wheat lasagna noodles
- 1 jar (25 to 28 ounces) vegan marinara sauce
- 8 ounces Italian-flavored ground seitan (see notes)
- 1 medium zucchini or yellow summer squash, shredded
- ¼ teaspoon crushed red pepper
- 1 cup shredded vegan cheese (optional)

Preheat the oven to 375 degrees F.

To make the *Spicy Tofu Ricotta*, put the tofu, lemon juice, Italian seasoning, garlic powder, cayenne pepper and salt into a medium-sized bowl and mash with a potato masher or large fork until the mixture has the consistency of ricotta cheese. Let stand for 5 to 10 minutes.

Meanwhile, to prepare the noodles, bring a large pot of salted water to a boil over medium-high heat. Add the noodles. Decrease the heat to medium-low and cook, stirring occasionally, until the noodles are *al dente*. Drain and rinse under cool water, then drain again.

Spread about ¾ cup of marinara sauce evenly over the bottom of a 13 by 9-inch or similar sized casserole dish. Arrange 4 lasagna noodles over the sauce. Spread the seitan over the noodles in an even layer. Top with ⅔ cup of sauce.

Spread all of the shredded zucchini over the sauce in an even layer and sprinkle with ¼ teaspoon crushed red pepper. Arrange 4 of the noodles over the zucchini. Spread all of the tofu ricotta over the noodles in an even layer, pressing it down with a rubber spatula to compress the lasagna and help hold it together. Arrange the remaining 4 noodles over the tofu. Spread the remaining marinara sauce over the noodles in an even layer.

Cover and bake for 60 to 65 minutes. Uncover and sprinkle with the optional vegan cheese, if desired. Bake uncovered for 5 to 7 minutes, until vegan cheese is melted.

Let cool for 15 minutes. Cut into 6 squares and serve warm.

CHEF'S NOTES:

- You may use Italian-style vegan "ground round" in place of the seitan.
- For a gluten-free option, use gluten-free lasagna noodles and replace the seitan with sautéed mushrooms. To make the mushrooms, put 8 to 10 ounces finely chopped mushrooms, ¼ cup water, 1 teaspoon olive oil, 1 teaspoon Italian seasoning blend and 1 teaspoon tamari into a sauté pan. Cover and cook over medium heat, stirring occasionally, for 7 to 10 minutes, until mushrooms are soft. Drain any excess liquid from the mushrooms and proceed with recipe as directed.

Orecchiette with Red Sweet Peppers, Escarole and Kalamata Sauce

MAKES 4 TO 6 SERVINGS

"Little Ear" pasta is smothered in a tangy sauce featuring escarole and sweet red peppers, then flavored with tangy Kalamata olives.

- ½ cup chopped scallions

- 2 teaspoons all-purpose seasoning

- ¼ teaspoon crushed red pepper

- ⅓ cup water, plus more as needed

- 3 red sweet bell peppers, chopped

- 1 jar (26 to 28 ounces) vegan marinara sauce

- 1 cup pitted Kalamata olives

- 1 small head escarole, thinly sliced

- 1 pound orecchiette pasta

Put the scallions, all-purpose seasoning, crushed red pepper and ⅓ cup water into a large skillet and cook over medium heat, stirring occasionally, for 3 to 4 minutes. Add the sweet peppers and a bit more water if the pan becomes dry. Cook, stirring occasionally, for 2 to 3 minutes. Decrease the heat to medium-low. Add the marinara sauce and olives. Cover and cook, stirring occasionally, for 10 to 12 minutes. Add the escarole, cover and cook, stirring occasionally, 3 to 5 minutes until the escarole is wilted and soft.

While the sauce cooks, bring a large pot of salted water to a boil over medium-high heat. Stir in the orecchiette. Decrease the heat to medium-low and cook, stirring occasionally, until just *al dente*. Drain the orecchiette.

For each serving, put some of the orecchiette in each of four to six pasta bowls, and top with a generous portion of the sauce. Serve immediately.

173

SAUCE

- 1 medium sweet onion, diced
- 3 tablespoons water, plus more if needed
- 1 tablespoon extra-virgin olive oil
- 2 teaspoons Italian seasoning blend
- 1 teaspoon tamari
- ¼ teaspoon crushed red pepper
- 8 ounces white button or cremini mushrooms, sliced
- 2 cloves garlic, minced
- 1 medium red or orange sweet bell pepper, seeded and diced
- 1 jar (24 to 26 ounces) vegan marinara sauce

TOFU RICOTTA

- 1 block (14 to 16 ounces) extra-firm regular tofu, drained
- 1 tablespoon extra-virgin olive oil
- 1 teaspoon tamari
- 1 teaspoon dried parsley
- 1 teaspoon Italian seasoning blend
- ½ teaspoon garlic powder
- Dash of cayenne pepper

NOODLES

- 22 to 24 lasagna noodles
- 1 tablespoon extra-virgin olive oil, plus more as needed

ADDITIONAL INGREDIENTS

- 2 small (or one large) zucchini, sliced into rounds
- Sea salt, to taste
- Freshly ground black pepper, to taste
- 1 cup shredded vegan cheese

Lasagna Muffin Cups

MAKES 6 TO 8 SERVINGS

If you want to impress your guests, serve them these splendid little lasagna cups. Baked in jumbo muffin tins, these appealing cups are filled with a flavorful sauce, layers of trimmed lasagna noodles and thin slices of fresh zucchini. This tasty entrée will certainly provide a *wow* factor at your supper table!

To make the sauce put the onion, 3 tablespoons water, 1 tablespoon olive oil, 2 teaspoons of Italian seasoning blend, 1 teaspoon tamari and crushed red pepper into a large skillet. Cover and cook over medium-low heat, stirring occasionally, for 10 minutes.

Add the mushrooms and garlic, cover and cook for 5 minutes, stirring occasionally, adding more water as needed if the pan becomes dry. Add the diced sweet pepper and the marinara sauce, cover and cook, stirring occasionally, for 25 to 35 minutes.

174

While the sauce cooks, make the tofu ricotta. Put the tofu, 1 tablespoon olive oil, 1 teaspoon tamari, parsley, 1 teaspoon Italian seasoning blend, garlic powder and dash of cayenne pepper into a large bowl, and mash with a potato masher or large fork, until the mixture resembles mashed ricotta cheese.

Meanwhile, prepare the noodles. Line two very large, rimmed cookie sheets with unbleached parchment paper. Bring a large pot of salted water to boil over medium-high heat. Decrease the heat to medium-low, add the lasagna noodles and cook them as the package suggests, making sure they are pliable, but still slightly *al dente*. Drain and cool the noodles immediately under cold running water.

Put a layer of noodles in a single layer on a lined cookie sheet. Brush the noodles with a thin layer of olive oil. Put a sheet of parchment paper over the first noodle layer. Continue with the remaining noodles in this manner. (If you are making the noodles a day ahead of time, wrap them tightly in plastic wrap at this point and refrigerate until using.)

Liberally coat two 6-cup jumbo muffin tins (see note on page 177) with vegan margarine. Line each cup with a 6 by 6-inch square of unbleached parchment paper, pressing it loosely into the cup and allowing a slight overhang on all sides of the cup.

Cut 10 to 12 of the noodles into 3 (or 4) pieces each, to make 36 small square "noodles" to use as the noodle layers in the lasagna cups. (Leave the remaining lasagna noodles whole.)

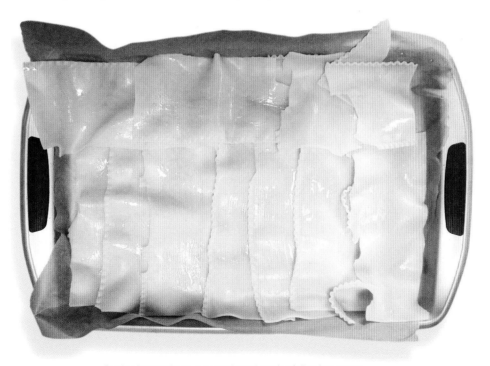

Recipe instructions are continued on the following page.

To assemble each cup, carefully curl a *whole* lasagna noodle around the inside perimeter of a lined muffin cup, trimming off the end and top, if needed, to fit into the cup. Then, gently press 1 of the small, pre-cut lasagna noodle squares into the muffin cup, fitting it snugly into the bottom of the cup. Repeat with the remaining 11 muffin cups.

Fill each lasagna cup as follows: spoon 2 heaping teaspoons of the sauce into the bottom of the cup, and top with 1 heaping teaspoon (or more) of the tofu ricotta and spread it in an even layer. In the following order, top with 1 small pre-cut lasagna noodle, 1 or 2 zucchini rounds, 1 heaping teaspoon of sauce, 1 small pre-cut noodle, 1 to 2 heaping teaspoons tofu ricotta, 1 small noodle, and finish with 2 heaping teaspoons sauce. Top each cup with several grinds of sea salt and freshly ground black pepper.

Cover the lasagna cups loosely with parchment paper and refrigerate for 1 to 4 hours, to allow them to firm up before baking. (You will have 12 lasagna cups in all.)

Preheat the oven to 375 degrees F. Tent the lasagna cups with foil, and bake for 45 to 50 minutes, or until heated through. Put the tins on a wire rack, remove the foil and top each of the cups with one-twelfth of the vegan cheese. Tent with foil, and bake an additional 10 to 15 minutes, or until the cheese is melted and lasagna cups are bubbling. Put the muffin tins on a wire rack and let cool for 10 to 12 minutes. Carefully lift the lasagna cups out of the tins, using the parchment paper as "handles." Carefully peel back the paper from each cup. Let cool 5 to 7 minutes. Serve 1 to 2 cups per person, with *Roasted Asparagus* (page 223) on the side.

CHEF'S NOTE: Each jumbo muffin cup generally holds about 1 cup of ingredients. Make certain to use a jumbo muffin tin with cups that are about 1 cup in size for this recipe.

Sensational Stuffed Manicotti

SAUCE

- 1 small sweet onion, chopped
- 2 tablespoons water, plus more as needed
- 1 tablespoon extra-virgin olive oil
- 1 teaspoon tamari
- 1 teaspoon Italian seasoning blend
- 3 cups sliced cremini mushrooms
- 1 large clove garlic, minced
- 1 jar (24 to 26 ounces) vegan marinara sauce
- ⅛ teaspoon crushed red pepper

MANICOTTI

- 1 block (14 to 16 ounces) extra-firm regular tofu, well drained
- 1 tablespoon extra-virgin olive oil
- 2 teaspoons tamari
- 1 teaspoon Italian seasoning blend
- 2 cloves garlic, chopped
- ½ cup chopped fresh parsley
- 12 manicotti shells, cooked *al dente* and cooled

TOPPING

- 2 slices Italian-style or whole-grain bread
- 1 teaspoon Italian seasoning blend
- 2 teaspoons extra-virgin olive oil, plus more as needed

FOR SERVING

- ½ jar (about 12 ounces) vegan marinara sauce
- Parsley sprigs and/or chopped fresh parsley

This manicotti is super yummy, and its classic taste and texture makes an enticing dish to serve at a casual gathering or weekend family meal.

Preheat the oven to 375 degrees F.

Put the onion, 2 tablespoons water, 1 tablespoon extra-virgin olive oil, 1 teaspoon tamari and 1 teaspoon Italian seasoning blend into a large skillet. Cover and cook 5 minutes, or until the onion begins to soften, stirring occasionally, adding more water 2 tablespoons at a time if the pan becomes dry.

Add the mushrooms, cover and cook for 5 minutes, stirring occasionally, adding more water 2 tablespoons at a time if the pan becomes dry. Add 1 clove minced garlic and cook for 2 to 3 minutes, stirring occasionally. Add the marinara sauce and crushed red pepper, cover and cook for 15 minutes.

While the sauce cooks, make the filling for the manicotti. Put the tofu, 1 tablespoon extra-virgin olive oil, 2 teaspoons tamari, 1 teaspoon Italian seasoning blend and 2 cloves minced garlic into a medium-sized bowl and mash using a potato masher or large fork until it has the consistency of ricotta cheese. Fold in the parsley.

Spread 1 cup of the sauce evenly over the bottom of a 12 by 9-inch or 13 by 9-inch casserole dish. Fill each manicotti shell with some of the filling, using a small spoon or tablespoon. Arrange the stuffed manicotti shells in a single layer in the prepared casserole dish. Tent with foil and bake for 35 minutes, or until bubbling.

178

While the manicotti bakes, make the topping. Tear the bread slices into small pieces. Put the bread pieces into a blender and process into coarse crumbs. Transfer the bread crumbs to a medium-sized bowl. Add the remaining topping ingredients and stir with a fork to combine. Add a bit more olive oil if the crumbs seem dry.

Remove the manicotti from the oven and put it on a wire rack. *Carefully* remove the foil (the manicotti will be *very* steamy and *very* hot!), and sprinkle the bread crumb mixture evenly over the top. Bake uncovered 10 to 15 minutes, or until the bread crumbs are slightly golden and filling is heated through. Cool 7 to 10 minutes.

Meanwhile, put about 12 ounces of marinara sauce into a small saucepan and bring to a simmer over medium heat. To serve, put a bit of marinara sauce on a plate and top with 2 pieces of manicotti (per person) and garnish with parsley sprigs. Offer extra marinara sauce on the side.

Tortilla Pizza Pie

These tasty pizza-style tortillas are quick to assemble and they're so tasty too! When you crave a pizza, but are short on time, these tantalizing pies will surely please.

- 4 whole-grain tortillas (gluten-free is fine)
- 12 ounces prepared vegan marinara sauce
- 1 teaspoon all-purpose seasoning
- ¼ teaspoon crushed red pepper
- ½ medium zucchini, grated
- 6 to 8 queen green olives, with pimento sliced
- ½ small sweet onion, diced
- 1½ cups bite-sized broccoli florets
- 8 heaping tablespoons shredded vegan cheese

Preheat the oven to 350 degrees F. Line two large, rimmed baking sheets with unbleached parchment paper.

Arrange 2 tortillas on each baking sheet. Top each tortilla with one-quarter of the marinara sauce, all-purpose seasoning and crushed red pepper. Spread one-quarter of the zucchini, olives, onion, broccoli florets and vegan cheese evenly over the top of each tortilla. Bake for 15 to 20 minutes, or until the vegan cheese is melted, tortillas are crisp and sauce is bubbling. Transfer the tortillas to wire racks and let cool for 5 minutes. Transfer each tortilla to a cutting board and cut into 4 slices. Serve 4 slices per person.

181

Cheeze-y Black Bean Tortilla Pizza

MAKES 2 TO 4 SERVINGS

This snazzy pizza preps for the oven in about 5 minutes,
using a few basic items you probably already have on hand,
making a *salsa-licious* lunch or quick supper.

- 4 corn, whole-grain or whole wheat tortillas (each 6-inches in diameter)

- 1 can (15 to 16 ounces) black beans, drained and rinsed

- ¼ teaspoon garlic powder

- ¼ teaspoon chili powder

- ¹⁄₁₆ heaping teaspoon cayenne pepper

- 7 tablespoons prepared salsa (mild, medium or hot), divided

- ⅔ cup shredded cheddar-style or jalapeño-style vegan cheese

- 2 cups firmly packed shredded romaine lettuce

Preheat the oven to 350 degrees F. Line a large, rimmed baking sheet (or two medium-sized sheets) with unbleached parchment paper. Arrange the tortillas in a single layer on the prepared baking sheet(s).

Put the black beans, garlic powder, chili powder, cayenne pepper and 3 tablespoons salsa into a medium-sized bowl and mash using a potato masher or large fork until combined. Divide the black bean mixture equally among the 4 tortillas and spread in an even layer, leaving a ½-inch "crust" around the perimeter of each tortilla. Top each tortilla with one-quarter of the vegan cheese.

Bake for 15 to 18 minutes, or until the tortillas are crisp and golden and bean mixture is heated through. Remove the pan from the oven and place it on a wire rack. Top the center of each pizza with 1 tablespoon of salsa.

To serve, arrange some of the lettuce on each of two to four plates and top each mound of lettuce with 1 or 2 pizzas. Serve immediately.

CHAPTER ELEVEN
Elegant Entrées

A delicious main dish is the cornerstone of a successful menu. Stuffed veggies, plant-based steaks, meatless loaves, bean burritos, hearty casseroles and more make wonderful centerpieces for a nourishing vegan meal. So whether you are serving these tasty dishes for a casual supper or elegant dinner party, remember: it's the entrée that's the true star of your menu!

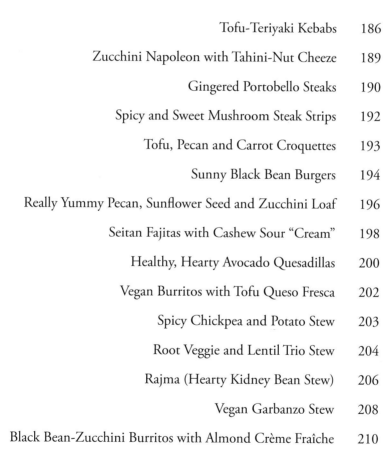

Recipes

185

Tofu-Teriyaki Kebabs

MAKES 6 TO 8 SERVINGS

KEBABS

- 12 to 16 bamboo skewers

- 2 medium red or orange sweet bell peppers, seeded and cut in chunks

- 1 large yellow or orange sweet bell pepper, seeded and cut in chunks

- 10 ounces cremini mushrooms, sliced in half (if large)

- 1 large (or 2 medium) zucchini, sliced

- 2 medium sweet onions, cut in chunks

- 1¾ cups grape tomatoes

- 3 tablespoons plus 1 teaspoon extra-virgin olive oil (see note), divided

- Several grinds freshly ground black pepper, to taste

- 2 packages (each 7 to 8 ounces, about 16 ounces in all) baked teriyaki-flavored tofu, cut in cubes (see note)

TERIYAKI SAUCE

- 3 tablespoons firmly packed dark brown sugar

- 3 tablespoons tamari

- 2 tablespoons extra-virgin olive oil

- 1 teaspoon garlic powder

I love the combination of colorful veggies slathered in a sweet homemade teriyaki sauce. The presentation of these enticing kebabs is supremely delightful, sure to please both omnivores and vegans alike.

Put the bamboo skewers in a shallow pan and top with about 1 inch of water. Allow to soak for 20 to 30 minutes. Preheat the oven to 375 degrees F. Line a very large, rimmed baking sheet with unbleached parchment paper.

Put the peppers, mushrooms, zucchini, onions and tomatoes into a large bowl. Drizzle 3 tablespoons of the olive oil over the veggies and top with several grinds of freshly ground black pepper. Toss gently with clean hands or a large spoon until all of the veggies are evenly coated with oil.

Put the tofu cubes into a small bowl. Top with 1 teaspoon olive oil. Toss gently to coat.

Evenly divide and thread the veggies and tofu onto the prepared skewers. Arrange the kebabs in a single layer on the lined baking sheet. Bake for 35 to 40 minutes.

Meanwhile, make the teriyaki sauce. Put the brown sugar, tamari, 2 tablespoons olive oil and garlic powder into a small bowl, and briskly whisk to combine (see note).

Remove the kebabs from the oven. Drizzle some of the sauce over each kebab, spreading it evenly over the top of the veggies and tofu. Return the kebabs to the oven and bake for an additional 15 to 20 minutes, or until the veggies are soft and edges of tofu are slightly browned and golden. To serve, put 2 skewers on each plate. Collect the sauce that has dripped to the bottom of the pan with a small spoon, and drizzle it over the top of each kebab. Serve with *Turmeric Quinoa* (page 237), *Spicy Rice* (page 233) or *Basic Quinoa* (page 237, see variation) on the side.

CHEF'S NOTES:

· You may also use plain extra-firm tofu that has been well-drained and pressed, cut into cubes and tossed with 2 teaspoons tamari and 1 teaspoon oil, in place of the baked teriyaki tofu, if desired. Proceed with recipe as directed.

· To lower the fat content of this recipe, you may use 2 tablespoons of olive oil to coat the veggies, instead of the 3 tablespoons.

· If you prefer extra sauce on your kebabs, simply double the sauce recipe. Proceed as directed.

Zucchini Napoleon with Tahini-Nut Cheeze

MAKES 6 SERVINGS

Ever come home from the farmer's market with a *huge* zucchini and can't figure out what to do with it? Elegant but easy, this tasty recipe uses a large zucchini to create a stunning entrée. Slices of tender squash are layered with a quick-to-prepare creamy and flavorful *Tahini-Nut Cheeze* (page 77), nestled atop a simple marinara.

- 1 very large zucchini (3 to 3½-inches in diameter at the wide end)
- 1¼ cups prepared vegan marinara sauce, divided, plus more as needed
- 1 recipe *Tahini-Nut Cheeze* (page 77)
- ¼ teaspoon sea salt, plus more to taste
- 3 large slices Italian-style bread, torn into chunks
- 1 teaspoon Italian seasoning blend
- 1 tablespoon extra-virgin olive oil

Preheat the oven to 375 degrees F.

Slice the large end of the zucchini into 12 slices, each about 3 to 3½-inches in diameter and ¼-inch thick. Slice 6 more slices from the zucchini, each about 2 to 2½-inches in diameter and ¼-inch thick.

Spread 1 cup of the marinara sauce in the bottom of a 9 by 12-inch or similar sized casserole. Arrange the 6 largest zucchini slices in a single layer over top of the sauce. Spread each slice with a generous amount of the *cheeze*. Sprinkle each slice with a dash of sea salt. Top with 6 more zucchini slices and spread each with generous amount of the *cheeze*. Sprinkle each slice with a dash of sea salt. Top each stack with a smaller zucchini slice, and spoon about 2 teaspoons of marinara sauce over the top of each napoleon. Tent with foil, and bake for 35 minutes.

While the napoleons bake, make the bread crumb topping. Put the bread chunks, Italian seasoning and ¼ teaspoon sea salt into a blender and process into coarse crumbs. Transfer the bread crumbs to a small bowl. Add the olive oil and stir to thoroughly coat the bread crumbs.

Remove the napoleons from the oven, uncover and sprinkle the bread crumb mixture over the top. Bake uncovered for an additional 10 to 12 minutes, or until the topping is crisp and zucchini is tender, checking often and adding a bit more marinara sauce to the bottom of the casserole dish, if it is becoming dry.

Put the casserole on a wire rack and let cool 5 to 7 minutes. Serve 1 napoleon per person, surrounded by pasta, quinoa or brown rice with a bit of the sauce from the bottom of the casserole spooned over the top.

Gingered Portobello Steaks

MAKES 4 TO 6 SERVINGS

These delicious mushroom steaks taste and look much like a conventional steak, making a great substitute for a meat entrée. I like to serve this snazzy dish for dinner parties, but it is easy enough to make for a weeknight meal, too!

- 3½ tablespoons extra-virgin olive oil, divided, plus more as needed

- 6 large (or 8 medium) portobello mushrooms, washed and stems removed

- 2 tablespoons tamari

- 1 tablespoon finely minced fresh ginger

- 2 cloves garlic, minced

- 1 tablespoon maple syrup

- 1/16 teaspoon cayenne pepper

Line a rimmed baking sheet, large enough to accommodate a single layer of the mushrooms, with unbleached parchment paper.

Brush about ½ teaspoon olive oil (in a thin layer) on each mushroom cap, then flip the mushrooms over and arrange them gill-side up on the prepared baking sheet.

To make the marinade, put 2½ tablespoons of olive oil and the tamari into a small bowl and briskly whisk to combine. Add the ginger, garlic, maple syrup and cayenne pepper and whisk to combine. Spoon an equal amount (about 2 teaspoons or so) of the marinade evenly over the gills of each mushroom. Cover with foil and refrigerate for 30 minutes to 1 hour to let the flavors marry.

Preheat the oven to 375 degrees F. Bake the mushrooms for 35 to 50 minutes (see note) or until they are almost soft. Remove the foil and bake for an additional 10 to 12 minutes, or until the mushrooms are golden and becoming caramelized.

Let the mushrooms rest at room temperature for 5 minutes. Transfer each mushroom onto a cutting board and cut into thick slices, on the bias. Serve 1 to 2 mushrooms per person, with *Pretty Orange Mash-Up* (page 230) and *Roasted Asparagus* (page 223) on the side.

CHEF'S NOTE: Baking time will vary depending upon the thickness of your mushrooms. Thinner mushrooms will require a shorter baking time, while thicker mushrooms will need to bake longer.

Spicy and Sweet Mushroom Steak Strips

MAKES 2 TO 3 SERVINGS

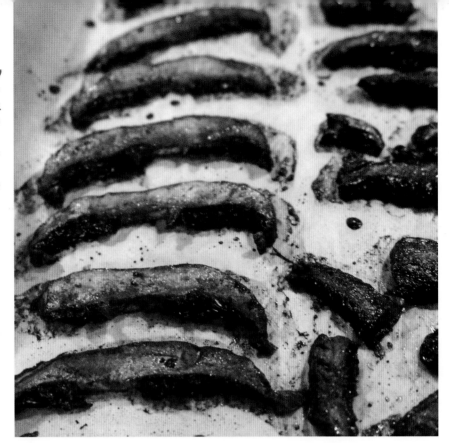

These meaty tasting "steak strips" really shine! Portobello mushrooms are marinated in a simple sauce, brimming with bold flavors. These strips can be served in many ways, over mashed potatoes, in a classic steak-style sandwich or arranged on top of a green salad. Mushroom lovers... rejoice!

- 3 large (or 4 small) portobello mushrooms, rinsed, patted dry and sliced into ¼ to ½-inch thick slices

- 1 tablespoon reduced-sodium tamari

- 2 teaspoons extra-virgin olive oil

- 2 teaspoons maple syrup

- ½ teaspoon garlic powder

- ¼ teaspoon cayenne pepper (use ⅛ teaspoon for less spicy)

Preheat the oven to 400 degrees F. Line a large, rimmed baking pan with unbleached parchment paper. Put the mushroom slices into a large bowl.

To make the sauce, put the tamari, olive oil, maple syrup, garlic powder and cayenne pepper in a small bowl and briskly whisk to combine.

Pour the sauce over the mushrooms and gently toss to coat. Arrange the mushroom slices in a single layer on the prepared pan. Brush any of the remaining sauce that has settled to the bottom of the bowl evenly over the mushroom slices.

Bake for 25 minutes. Put the pan on a wire rack, let cool 3 minutes and serve.

JAZZY TIP: Portobello mushrooms have a thick and tempting texture along with a rich taste that stands in well for meat in many recipes. Try using sliced portobellos as a replacement for meat in your favorite stew, pasta sauce, casserole, soup or stir-fry. They are great marinated and cooked whole on the grill too, in place of a meat-based burger. So versatile!

Tofu, Pecan and Carrot Croquettes

MAKES 8 CROQUETTES

While not a classic croquette per se, these dainty patties have a slightly crisp outside and a soft, tender inside that stands in beautifully for the traditional version. Pecans add texture and carrots provide moisture, while the tofu imparts a smooth texture.

- ½ block (7 to 8 ounces) extra-firm regular tofu, drained and lightly pressed

- 2 teaspoons reduced-sodium tamari

- 1½ teaspoons extra-virgin olive oil

- ¾ teaspoon chili powder

- ½ teaspoon garlic powder

- ½ teaspoon ground cumin

- 1 cup peeled and grated carrots

- ½ cup chopped pecans

- 2 heaping tablespoons sesame tahini, plus more as needed

Preheat the oven to 375 degrees F. Line a large, rimmed baking pan with unbleached parchment paper.

Put the tofu, tamari, olive oil, chili powder, garlic powder and cumin into a large bowl and mash using a potato masher or large fork until crumbly. Add the carrots and pecans, and stir with a large fork to combine. Add the tahini and combine using clean hands until the mixture holds together, adding more tahini if needed if the mixture seems too dry.

Using a ¼ cup measure, scoop up some of the croquette mixture and press it firmly into the cup, so it becomes compressed, then drop it onto the lined pan. Flatten slightly with a spatula. Continue in this manner with the remaining croquette mixture, until you have 8 croquettes.

Bake for 15 to 17 minutes or until slightly golden underneath. Carefully flip (the croquettes will be *very* soft) and bake for 12 to 17 minutes more, or until crisp and golden on the outside. Cool for 5 minutes. These are delicious served with a baked sweet potato, *Lemon-Sesame Broccoli* (page 214) and *Quick Catsup-Mayo* (page 75) on the side.

Tired of frozen meat-free burgers? These burgers bring a ray of sunshine to your table, with protein-rich ingredients like black beans, sunflower seeds and walnuts. A cross between a hearty burger and flavorful paté, these patties prep for the oven in less than 10 minutes, making them an ideal option for a casual weekday meal.

194

- ½ cup roasted and salted sunflower seeds

- ½ cup chopped walnut halves

- 1 cup lightly packed, fresh whole-grain bread crumbs (see note)

- 2 teaspoons extra-virgin olive oil, plus more as needed

- 1 can (15 to 16 ounces) black beans, drained and rinsed

- 5 tablespoons marinara sauce, plus more as needed

- 3 tablespoons minced fresh onion

- ½ teaspoon garlic powder

- ½ teaspoon Italian seasoning blend

Sunny Black Bean Burgers

MAKES 6 SERVINGS

L ine a medium-sized baking pan with unbleached parchment paper.

Put the sunflower seeds into a blender and process into coarse crumbs. Transfer to a small bowl. Put the walnuts into a blender and process into coarse crumbs and add them to the ground sunflower seeds. Add the bread crumbs to the sunflower seed/walnut mixture and stir using a large spoon to thoroughly combine. Pour in the olive oil and stir to combine, adding a bit more olive oil (up to 1 more teaspoon), if the mixture seems dry.

Put the black beans, marinara sauce, onion, garlic powder and Italian seasoning into a medium-sized bowl and lightly mash, using a potato masher or large fork. Stir in the nut/bread crumb mixture and mix together until well combined, adding a bit more of the marinara sauce if the mixture seems dry. The mixture should hold together when gathered in the palm of your hand.

To form a burger, scoop up a scant ½ cup of the mixture and drop it onto the lined pan. Gently form it into the shape of a burger. Continue in this manner until you have formed 6 burgers. Refrigerate for about 30 minutes (or up to 2 hours) to allow the burgers to firm up.

Preheat the oven to 375 degrees F. Bake for 30 to 35 minutes, or until slightly golden, flipping the burgers half way through cooking. Put the pan on a wire rack and let cool (to firm up) for 5 to 10 minutes before serving. (These burgers will be slightly soft, so handle them carefully!) Serve on whole-grain buns, with lettuce and tomatoes, topped with *Quick Marinara-Mayo Sauce* (page 75, see variation). Serve *Russet Oven Fries* (page 232) or *Colorful Confetti Fries* (page 234) on the side.

CHEF'S NOTE: Freshly made bread crumbs *must* be used in this recipe, as dry bread crumbs will not hold the burgers together. To make fresh bread crumbs, tear 2 to 3 slices of fresh, whole-grain bread into chunks. Put the bread chunks into a blender and process into coarse crumbs.

Really Yummy Pecan, Sunflower Seed and Zucchini Loaf

- 1½ cups raw unsalted sunflower seeds
- 1 cup pecan halves
- 1 teaspoon Italian seasoning blend
- ¾ teaspoon sea salt, divided
- 2 cups fresh bread crumbs (see note)
- ⅓ cup finely minced red onion
- 2 cups firmly packed grated zucchini
- 1½ tablespoons extra-virgin olive oil, plus more as needed

Oh yeah! When you need a tasty and satisfying meatless loaf, this easy-to-prepare vegan version will truly please!

Lightly coat an 8 by 4-inch loaf pan with vegan margarine. Line the pan with unbleached parchment paper, leaving an overhang of 2½-inch "wings" on the two lengthwise sides of the pan. Put the sunflower seeds, pecans, Italian seasoning and ¼ teaspoon sea salt into a blender and process into coarse crumbs. Transfer the mixture to a large bowl. Add the bread crumbs, ½ teaspoon sea salt and the minced onion and stir to combine. Add the grated zucchini and olive oil and stir to combine. Add a bit more olive oil, if the mixture seems dry.

Press the mixture into the prepared loaf pan and smooth the top. Fold the excess parchment paper over the top of the loaf and gently press it down. This will keep the loaf moist while baking. If time allows, refrigerate for 2 to 4 hours to allow the loaf to firm up before baking.

Preheat the oven to 375 degrees F. Bake for 45 to 55 minutes, or until the center of the loaf is heated through. Remove the loaf from the oven and carefully peel back the parchment paper that is covering the top of the loaf. Bake for an additional 15 to 20 minutes, or until the top of the loaf is slightly golden in color, firm to the touch and heated through.

Put the pan on a wire rack and let cool 10 minutes. Using the parchment paper "wings," carefully lift the loaf from the pan and put it on the wire rack. Carefully peel off the parchment paper. Let cool 5 to 10 minutes more. Gently cut the loaf into 6 to 8 thick slices (the loaf will be soft!), using a serrated bread knife. Wipe the knife clean after cutting each slice. Serve 1 to 2 slices per person, with *Red Potato and Cauliflower Mash* (page 230), *Broccoli with Maple-Tamari Sauce* (page 214) or *Lemon-Sesame Broccoli* (page 214) and *Simple Mushroom Gravy* (page 76) on the side.

CHEF'S NOTES:

- Freshly made bread crumbs must be used in this recipe, as dry bread crumbs will not hold the loaf together. To make fresh bread crumbs, tear 4 to 6 slices of fresh, soft whole-grain bread into chunks. Put one-half of the bread chunks into a blender and process into coarse crumbs. Repeat with the remaining bread chunks.
- You may use whole-grain, whole wheat, gluten-free or your preferred variety of fresh bread in this recipe.

Seitan Fajitas with Cashew Sour "Cream"

MAKES 4 SERVINGS

FAJITAS

- 1 large sweet onion, sliced

- ¼ cup water, plus more as needed

- 2 teaspoons extra-virgin olive oil, divided, plus more as needed

- 2 teaspoons tamari, divided, plus more as needed

- 1 teaspoon chili powder

- ¼ teaspoon ground cumin

- ¼ teaspoon garlic powder

- ⅛ to ¼ teaspoon crushed red pepper, to taste

- ¼ cup diced celery

- 3 very large (or 4 medium) yellow, orange or red sweet bell peppers, seeded and sliced

- 8 to 10 ounces "chicken-style" seitan strips, or plant-based protein of your choice (see note)

- 4 whole-grain or habanero-lime tortillas (each 10 to 11-inches in diameter)

CASHEW SOUR CREAM

- ⅔ cup chopped raw cashews

- ½ cup water, plus more as needed

- 2 tablespoons lemon juice

- Dash of sea salt, to taste

These flavorful vegan fajitas feature the meaty texture of seitan drizzled with a delicious cashew sour cream. So good!

To make the fajitas, put the onion, ¼ cup water, 1 teaspoon olive oil, 1 teaspoon tamari, chili powder, cumin, garlic powder and crushed red pepper into a large skillet. Cover and cook over medium heat, stirring occasionally, for 5 minutes.

Decrease the heat to medium-low, add the celery, cover and cook, stirring occasionally, for 5 to 7 minutes. Add a bit more water, if needed, if the pan becomes dry. Add the sweet peppers, 1 teaspoon olive oil, 1 teaspoon tamari and the seitan strips and a bit more water or olive oil if the pan has become dry. Cover and cook, stirring occasionally, for 5 to 7 minutes, or until the peppers are soft and the seitan strips are heated through. Taste and add more tamari, if desired, and cook for 1 minute more.

198

While the seitan mixture cooks, preheat the oven to 350 degrees F. Wrap the tortillas in foil and bake for 4 to 6 minutes, or until *just* warmed.

Meanwhile, make the cashew sour cream. Put the cashews, ½ cup water, lemon juice and dash of sea salt into a high-performance blending appliance, and blend until smooth and creamy, adding up to 2 additional tablespoons water if a thinner consistency is preferred.

To serve the fajitas, put a warm tortilla on a large plate. Put one-quarter of the seitan mixture on one side of the warm tortilla, then fold the other half of the tortilla over the seitan mixture. Generously drizzle with some of the cashew sour cream (see note). Continue with the remaining tortillas, seitan mixture and cashew sour cream to make 4 fajitas. Serve with *Spicy Rice* (page 233) on the side, drizzled with more of the cashew cream and garnished with chopped scallions, if desired.

CHEF'S NOTES:

· Many varieties of plant-based protein work well in this dish. You may use any meat analog, such as plain seitan or vegan sausages, or you can use cooked white beans, black beans or extra-firm regular tofu (that has been drained, pressed and cubed) or cubed tempeh in place of the "chicken-style" seitan, if you like.

· If you have some Cashew Sour Cream leftover, store tightly covered in the refrigerator for up to 2 days.

Healthy, Hearty Avocado Quesadillas

MAKES 4 SERVINGS

These satisfying quesadillas make a hearty offering for a filling lunch or light supper. The creaminess of the avocado stands in for some of the cheese, while kale and romaine lettuce make a nutritious addition to these tasty quesadillas.

- 4 whole-grain or whole wheat tortillas (each 10 to 11-inches in diameter)

- 2 large avocados, peeled, pitted and sliced

- 1½ cups firmly packed, thinly sliced kale, remove stems before chopping

- 1½ cups firmly packed, thinly sliced romaine lettuce, plus more for serving

- 2 small tomatoes, thinly sliced

- 8 heaping tablespoons prepared salsa, plus more for serving

- 4 heaping tablespoons vegan cheese (optional)

- ½ red sweet bell pepper, diced (for serving)

Preheat the oven to 350 degrees F. Line a large, rimmed baking pan with unbleached parchment paper.

To assemble the first quesadilla, put a tortilla on a large dinner plate. On one side of the tortilla, layer one-quarter of the avocado slices, one-quarter of the kale, one-quarter of the romaine lettuce, one-quarter of the tomato slices, 2 heaping tablespoons prepared salsa and 1 heaping tablespoon of the optional vegan cheese. Fold the other half of the tortilla over the filling and gently press down so the tortilla becomes slightly compressed and holds together while cooking. Carefully transfer the tortilla to the lined pan.

Repeat the process to assemble the remaining quesadillas. Loosely cover the tortillas with a piece of unbleached parchment paper and then tent with foil. (This will keep the quesadillas from drying out as they bake.)

Bake for 20 to 25 minutes. Remove from oven and carefully uncover the quesadillas (the steam will be *very* hot!) and bake an additional 5 to 10 minutes or until the quesadillas are slightly crisp and golden on top. Put the pan on a wire rack. Let cool for 5 to 7 minutes. To serve, top each quesadilla with more romaine lettuce and some diced pepper, with extra salsa on the side (see note).

CHEF'S NOTE: If desired, you can drizzle either *Cashew Sour Cream* (page 198) or *Almond Crème Fraîche* (page 210) over the top of the quesadillas before serving.

Vegan Burritos with Tofu Queso Fresca

MAKES 4 SERVINGS

TOFU QUESO FRESCA

- ½ block (7 to 8 ounces) extra-firm regular tofu, drained
- ¼ teaspoon garlic powder
- ¼ teaspoon ground turmeric
- ¼ teaspoon dried oregano
- ¼ teaspoon ground cumin
- ¼ teaspoon chili powder
- ¼ teaspoon sea salt

BURRITO

- 4 large whole-grain tortillas (each 10 to 11-inches in diameter)
- 1 can (15 to 16 ounces) black beans, drained and rinsed
- 2 cups baby spinach, chopped
- ½ medium tomato, diced
- 8 tablespoons jarred "hot" salsa, plus more for serving (see note)

TOPPINGS (optional)

- *Cashew Sour Cream* (page 198)
- Chopped scallions
- Chopped fresh cilantro or parsley

When you crave a Mexican-inspired meal, these easy-to-make burritos will truly satisfy. A spicy *queso fresco-style* tofu *cheeze* takes the place of dairy cheese, complemented by tender baby spinach, black beans and spicy salsa to make a delicious, one-dish meal.

Preheat the oven to 375 degrees F. Line a 9 by 12-inch or similar sized baking dish with aluminum foil, allowing a 5-inch overhang on the two lengthwise sides of the dish. Line the foil with unbleached parchment paper, allowing a 5-inch overhang on the two lengthwise sides of the dish.

To make the *Tofu Queso Fresca*, put the tofu, garlic powder, turmeric, oregano, cumin, chili powder and sea salt into a large bowl and mash using a potato masher or large fork until crumbly.

To assemble the first burrito, put a tortilla on a large dinner plate. On one side of the tortilla, layer one-quarter of the tofu mixture, one-quarter of the beans, one-quarter of the spinach, one-quarter of the tomatoes and 2 tablespoons of salsa. Roll the tortilla tightly around the filling and place it seam-side down in the prepared baking dish. Repeat the process to assemble the remaining burritos.

Bring the sides of the parchment paper over the burritos, fold over and seal tightly. Bring the sides of the foil over the parchment and crimp to seal. (This will keep the burritos from drying out as they bake.)

Bake for 30 minutes, or until heated through. Remove from oven and carefully uncover the burritos (the steam will be *very* hot!) and bake, uncovered, for an additional 5 to 10 minutes, or until the edges of the burritos are slightly crisp and filling is bubbly and hot. Remove from oven and let stand 5 to 7 minutes, to cool slightly before serving. Garnish with optional toppings, if desired, and serve extra salsa on the side.

CHEF'S NOTE: For less spicy burritos, use a mild or medium prepared salsa in place of the hot salsa.

Spicy Chickpea and Potato Stew

MAKES 6 SERVINGS

This sensational stew is very easy to prepare and has a real kick to it, with a bit of an Indian flair.

- ½ large red onion, diced

- 1 cup water

- 1 teaspoon tamari

- 3 cups quartered baby red potatoes (peeling is optional)

- 1½ cups carrots, sliced (peeling is optional)

- 2 cups chopped tomatoes

- 1 large clove garlic, minced

- 1 teaspoon ground cumin

- ½ teaspoon ground turmeric

- ½ teaspoon chili powder

- ½ teaspoon dried cilantro

- ⅛ teaspoon sea salt, plus more as needed

- ⅛ teaspoon freshly ground black pepper

- 1 can (15 to 16 ounces) chickpeas (garbanzo beans), drained and rinsed

- 2 cups bite-sized cauliflower florets

- 1 cup green beans, trimmed and cut into 1½-inch pieces

- 1½ cups peeled and diced sweet potatoes

Put the onion, water and tamari into a large soup pot. Cover and cook over medium heat for 2 minutes, stirring occasionally. Decrease the heat to medium-low. Add the potatoes, carrots and tomatoes. Cover and cook, stirring occasionally, for 5 minutes. Add the garlic, cumin, turmeric, chili powder, cilantro, sea salt and black pepper and bring to a simmer. Cover and cook for 2 minutes. Add the chickpeas, cauliflower, green beans and sweet potatoes. Add a bit more water, if needed, to cover the vegetables by about ½-inch. Cover and simmer for 30 to 35 minutes, stirring occasionally, until all the veggies are soft and stew has thickened. Serve with *Spicy Rice* (page 233) or *Turmeric Quinoa* (page 237) on the side.

Root Veggie and Lentil Trio Stew

MAKES 6 SERVINGS

The satisfying combo of my favorite root vegetables, combined with a lively lentil trio, makes a hearty and filling stew. Serve it with warm, crusty bread for a delicious and satisfying *one-bowl* meal.

- 1½ cups lentil trio blend, picked over, rinsed well (see note)
- 4 medium carrots, peeled and thickly sliced
- 4 medium russet potatoes, peeled and cubed
- 2 large sweet potatoes, peeled and cubed
- 1 can (26 to 28 ounces) diced fire-roasted tomatoes, with juice (see note)
- 6 cups water
- 1 medium clove garlic, minced
- 1 large vegan bouillon cube, crumbled
- 1 teaspoon tamari
- 2 teaspoons extra-virgin olive oil
- ½ teaspoon garam masala (see note)
- Sea salt, to taste
- Freshly ground black pepper, to taste

Put all of the ingredients into a large soup pot and stir to combine. Cover and bring to a simmer over medium heat. Decrease the heat to medium-low, cover and cook, stirring occasionally, for 35 to 45 minutes, or until the root vegetables and the lentils are soft. Season with salt and pepper, to taste. Spoon into deep bowls and serve with *Festive Kale-Cranberry Salad* or *Baby Kale, Carrot and Cranberry Salad* (page 105) on the side.

CHEF'S NOTES:

- If you cannot find a pre-packaged lentil trio blend, you may use any combination of black beluga, red and/or green lentils. Alternately, you may combine and use two or three of your favorite lentil varieties in this recipe.
- If you cannot find fire-roasted tomatoes, you may substitute regular canned diced tomatoes.
- For a spicier stew, use 1 teaspoon garam masala.

Rajma (Hearty Kidney Bean Stew)

MAKES 4 SERVINGS

This awesome recipe was created by writer-director-producer Sri Rao, and he was kind enough to share it with us on the *Jazzy Vegetarian* television show this season! It's hard to believe that simple kidney beans can transform into a dish with so many layers of flavor. Smoky cumin, earthy coriander, warm ginger and spicy garlic combine to make *Rajma*, a true showstopper. This is North Indian comfort food—and all you'll need is one bowl of warm stew to understand why.

- 1 tablespoon extra-light olive oil or canola oil
- 1 teaspoon black mustard seeds
- 1 medium onion, finely chopped
- 1 tablespoon minced garlic
- ½ tablespoon grated fresh ginger
- 2 teaspoons ground cumin
- 1 teaspoon Indian red chili powder or cayenne pepper
- 1 teaspoon salt, plus more as needed
- ¼ teaspoon ground turmeric
- 2 medium tomatoes, diced
- 2 cans (15.5-ounces each) red kidney beans, drained and rinsed
- 1 cup hot water
- 1¼ tablespoons freshly squeezed lemon juice or ¼ teaspoon tamarind paste
- ½ tablespoon tamari or soy sauce
- 2 tablespoons chopped cilantro
- 1 teaspoon ground coriander
- Chopped fresh cilantro, for garnish (optional)
- Vegan yogurt or *Cashew Sour Cream* (page 198) to finish (optional)

In a medium-sized saucepan, heat the oil over medium-high heat. Once the oil is shimmering hot, add the mustard seeds. As soon as the seeds begin to pop, add the onion and cook, stirring, for about 3 minutes, reducing the heat to medium (or medium-low), if necessary, to prevent the onions from burning. Add the garlic and ginger and cook, stirring, for another minute. Add the cumin, Indian red chili powder (or cayenne pepper), salt and turmeric. Stir the spices into the onions, allowing them to bloom, for about 30 seconds.

Stir in the tomatoes. Cover and cook until the tomatoes have broken down, 5 to 7 minutes.

Add the beans and stir. Add the water and bring to a boil. Add the lemon juice (or tamarind paste) into the hot stew along with the tamari (or soy sauce). Reduce heat, cover and simmer for 30 minutes, stirring occasionally.

Add the cilantro and coriander. Use the back of a large spoon or a potato masher to crush about half of the beans to create a rich gravy. Continue cooking, increasing heat as necessary, until the sauce is thick and transforms from red to deep brown, another 5 to 10 minutes or so.

Adjust the salt and seasonings, to taste. Garnish with optional fresh cilantro and serve in a bowl with *Turmeric Quinoa* (page 237), *Spicy Rice* (page 233) or roti (Indian flatbread). If desired, finish with a dollop of vegan yogurt or *Cashew Sour Cream* (page 198).

Reprinted with permission from *Bollywood Kitchen: Home-Cooked Indian Meals Paired With Unforgettable Bollywood Films* by Sri Rao (Houghton Mifflin Harcourt, 2017).

Photo by Sidney Bensimon. Sri Rao is a writer-director-producer living in New York City. Learn more about Sri at: www.NewYorkSri.com

Vegan Garbanzo Stew

MAKES 6 SERVINGS

This hearty and comforting stew has a spicy kick that gives it real jazzy pizzazz! The vegan "sausage" adds classic texture and the *Jazzy Sazón* (page 81) provides an authentic taste. This stew is delicious served over *Spicy Rice* (page 233) with a green salad on the side to make a truly satisfying meal.

- 1 medium sweet onion, chopped
- 1 tablespoon *Jazzy Sazón* (page 81), divided
- 2 teaspoons extra-virgin olive oil, divided
- ½ cup water
- 2 cups vegetable broth, divided
- 2 cups peeled and cubed red or white potatoes
- 1 large red or yellow sweet bell pepper, seeded and chopped
- 1 small green bell pepper, seeded and chopped
- 2 large cloves garlic, minced
- 2 cans (15 to 16 ounces each) chickpeas (garbanzo beans), drained and rinsed
- 14 ounces vegan sausage, sliced (see note)
- 10 green queen olives with pimento, diced
- 1 can (26 to 28 ounces) diced tomatoes, with juice
- ⅛ teaspoon cayenne pepper
- Sea salt, to taste

Put the onion, 1 teaspoon *Jazzy Sazón*, 1 teaspoon olive oil and ½ cup water into a large soup pot. Cover and cook 7 minutes, stirring occasionally. Add 1 cup vegetable broth, potatoes, sweet bell pepper, green bell pepper, garlic, 1 teaspoon *Jazzy Sazón* and 1 teaspoon olive oil. Cover and let cook 15 minutes, stirring occasionally. Stir in the garbanzo beans, vegan sausage and olives. Add the diced tomatoes, 1 cup vegetable broth, 1 teaspoon *Jazzy Sazón* and cayenne pepper and stir to combine. Cover and cook 35 to 45 minutes, or until vegetables are soft. Season with salt, to taste. Serve over *Spicy Rice* (page 233).

CHEF'S NOTE: If you prefer not to use a meat analog, increase the potatoes to 3 cups and increase the garbanzo beans to about 2⅔ cans. Proceed with recipe as directed.

Black Bean-Zucchini Burritos with Almond Crème Fraîche

MAKES 2 TO 4 SERVINGS

These cheeseless burritos get their zing from shredded zucchini and spicy salsa. Topped with a vegan almond cream, these burritos are easy to prepare and super satisfying to serve.

BURRITOS

- 1 can (15 to 16 ounces) black beans, drained and rinsed
- 5 tablespoons prepared salsa, plus more as needed
- 1⅔ cups shredded zucchini (about 2 small), divided
- 1½ teaspoons chili powder
- 4 whole-grain tortillas (each about 10-inches in diameter)

ALMOND CREME FRAICHE

- ½ cup raw almonds
- 6 tablespoons water, plus more as needed
- 2 tablespoons freshly squeezed lemon juice

GARNISH

- 8 cherry or grape tomatoes, thinly sliced

Preheat the oven to 350 degrees F. Line a 9 by 12-inch or similar sized baking dish with aluminum foil, allowing a 5-inch overhang on the two lengthwise sides of the dish. Line the foil with unbleached parchment paper, allowing a 5-inch overhang on the two lengthwise sides of the dish.

Put the black beans and salsa into a medium-sized bowl and lightly mash, using a potato masher or large fork until well combined but still chunky. Put 1⅓ cups of the shredded zucchini and the chili powder into a separate medium-sized bowl and gently toss to coat.

To assemble the first burrito, put 1 tortilla on a large dinner plate. Put one-quarter of the black bean mixture in the center of the tortilla. Top with ⅓ cup of the shredded zucchini/chili powder mixture. Roll the tortilla up around the filling, folding in the sides, as you go, to make a burrito. Put the burrito seam-side down on the lined pan. Repeat the process to assemble the remaining 3 burritos.

Bring the sides of the parchment paper over the burritos, and fold it over. Bring the sides of the foil over the parchment and crimp to seal. (This will keep the burritos from drying out as they bake.) Bake for 40 to 45 minutes,

or until heated through. Remove from oven and carefully uncover the burritos (the steam will be very hot!). Bake for 5 minutes more, or until the edges and tops of the tortillas are slightly golden. Put the pan on a wire rack and let cool 5 minutes before serving.

Meanwhile, to make the *Almond Crème Fraîche*, put the almonds, water and lemon juice into a blender and process until smooth and creamy, adding more water, as needed, to achieve the desired consistency.

To serve, put 1 or 2 burrito(s) on a plate. Garnish each burrito with one-quarter of the remaining shredded zucchini and arrange several cherry tomato slices on the side. Drizzle one-quarter of the *Almond Crème Fraîche* over the top. For a satisfying meal, serve with *Turmeric Quinoa* (page 237) on the side.

CHAPTER TWELVE
Jazzin' Up Veggies and Grains

Fresh vegetables and whole grains are often the star of a plant-based menu, but in this chapter I'll share some of my favorite ways to serve these nutrient dense foods as a side dish. Featuring root veggies, green veggies and rainbow colored veggies, along with festive grains, these sassy recipes will wake up any meal you may be serving.

Recipes

Broccoli with Maple-Tamari Sauce

MAKES 4 SERVINGS

Tender broccoli florets, combined with a salty and sweet sauce, make a satisfying companion to any healthful supper.

- 5 cups bite-sized broccoli florets
- 2 teaspoons reduced-sodium or regular tamari
- 2 teaspoons maple syrup
- 1 teaspoon extra-virgin olive oil
- ¹⁄₁₆ to ⅛ teaspoon cayenne pepper

Fit a steamer basket into a large pot with a tight-fitting lid. Add 2 to 3 inches of cold water, then add the broccoli florets. Cover, bring to a boil and steam for 6 to 8 minutes, or until crisp tender. Put the tamari, maple syrup, olive oil and cayenne pepper into a small bowl and briskly whisk until well combined. Transfer the broccoli to a medium-sized bowl and pour the sauce over the broccoli. Gently toss to coat. Serve immediately.

Lemon-Sesame Broccoli

MAKES 2 TO 3 SERVINGS

With a tasty sweet and sour sauce, this inviting way to serve broccoli is easy, low in fat *and* delicious. The cayenne pepper gives it a real kick, but if you prefer a non-spicy sauce, just leave it out.

- 6 cups bite-sized broccoli florets
- 1½ tablespoons maple syrup, plus more as needed
- 1 tablespoon freshly squeezed lemon juice, plus more as needed
- ¼ teaspoon reduced-sodium or regular tamari
- 1 small clove garlic, minced
- 1 teaspoon raw or roasted sesame seeds
- ¹⁄₁₆ to ⅛ teaspoon cayenne pepper

Fit a steamer basket into a large pot with a tight-fitting lid. Add 2 to 3 inches of cold water, then add the broccoli florets. Cover, bring to a boil and steam for 6 to 8 minutes, or until crisp tender.

While the florets cook, put the maple syrup, lemon juice, tamari, garlic, sesame seeds and cayenne pepper into a small bowl and briskly whisk to combine. Taste, and add more maple syrup or lemon juice, if desired. Transfer the hot broccoli to a medium-sized bowl and pour the sauce over the florets. Gently stir to coat and serve.

Festive Broccoli Stir-Fry

MAKES 4 SERVINGS

This festive array of colorful veggies and garbanzo beans is sautéed in olive oil and flavored with a bit of spice, making a lively entrée for a light meal or a fabulous side dish for a company supper.

- 7 cups bite-sized broccoli florets
- 1 tablespoon extra-virgin olive oil
- 3 teaspoons reduced-sodium or regular tamari, divided
- ¼ teaspoon crushed red pepper
- 2 tablespoons water, plus more as needed
- 1 can (15 to 16 ounces) chickpeas (garbanzo beans), drained and rinsed
- 1 large red or yellow sweet bell pepper, seeded and sliced
- 1 clove garlic, minced
- Sea salt, to taste
- Freshly ground black pepper, to taste

Put the broccoli florets, olive oil, 2 teaspoons tamari, crushed red pepper and 2 tablespoons water into a large sauté pan. Cover and cook over medium heat for 3 to 5 minutes, stirring occasionally, adding more water as the pan becomes dry.

Decrease the heat to medium-low. Add the chickpeas, sweet pepper, garlic and 1 teaspoon tamari. Cover and cook, stirring occasionally, for 3 to 6 minutes, or until the broccoli is crisp tender and the chickpeas are heated through. Season with salt and pepper, to taste.

215

Cashew Stuffed Artichokes

MAKES 4 TO 8 SERVINGS

You know how I adore artichokes. I have loved 'em since I was a little girl and whenever I see beautiful varieties in my marketplace, I cannot resist them. This recipe is festive and filling with cashews and sunflower seeds showcased in a flavorful stuffing. I like to serve this colorful dish as a first course, or they do double duty as a luncheon entrée.

- 1 can (26 to 28 ounces) diced tomatoes, with juice
- 2 large cloves garlic, minced
- 2 slices whole-grain bread, torn into chunks
- ⅓ cup chopped raw or roasted cashews
- ¼ cup roasted, salted sunflower seeds
- 1 tablespoon fresh chopped basil, or 1 teaspoon dried basil
- ¼ teaspoon Italian seasoning blend
- ¼ teaspoon sea salt
- 1 tablespoon extra-virgin olive oil
- ¾ cup diced fresh tomatoes
- 4 medium trimmed and cooked artichokes (see trimming and cooking instructions in *Chilled Artichokes with Lemon-Mayo Dipping Sauce* recipe, page 218), cut in half, with choke removed (see note)

Preheat the oven to 400 degrees F. Spread the canned tomatoes with juice over the bottom of a 9 by 12-inch or similar sized casserole dish. Sprinkle the minced garlic evenly over the tomatoes.

Put the bread, cashews, sunflower seeds, basil, Italian seasoning and sea salt into a blender or food processor and process into coarse crumbs. Transfer to a medium-sized bowl. Add the olive oil and stir to combine. Add the fresh tomatoes and gently stir, until thoroughly combined.

Arrange the artichoke halves, cut-side up, on top of the tomatoes and garlic in the prepared casserole dish. Stuff each cavity with one-eighth of the cashew/sunflower seed mixture. Cover with foil and bake for 40 to 45 minutes. Uncover and bake for 10 minutes, or until the top of the stuffing is golden brown.

To serve, put some of the tomato sauce from the bottom of the casserole dish on each of eight individual serving plates and top it with 1 stuffed artichoke half (see note). Serve warm or cover, refrigerate and serve cold.

CHEF'S NOTES:

- Once the artichokes are cooked and cooled, you can remove the "choke." Begin by cutting each artichoke in half, vertically. Scoop out the fuzzy center choke with a grapefruit spoon or teaspoon. If you are cooking the artichokes ahead of time, wrap the artichokes tightly in plastic wrap and refrigerate for up to 1 day before preparing this recipe.

- If you are serving this as a luncheon entrée, serve 2 artichoke halves per person.

Chilled Artichokes with Lemon-Mayo Dipping Sauce

MAKES 4 SERVINGS

A lovely dish to serve as an elegant first course or a tempting side dish, these artichokes look as good as they taste—which is sensational!

ARTICHOKES

- 4 small to medium artichokes
- 1 teaspoon balsamic vinegar (optional)

DIPPING SAUCE

- 3 tablespoons vegan mayonnaise
- 1 tablespoon freshly squeezed lemon juice

GARNISH

- Dash chili powder, for garnish
- Dash Italian seasoning blend, for garnish

To trim and clean the artichokes, start by cutting off the top ½ to 1 inch of each artichoke to remove the spiky tips. Cut off any remaining spiky tips with kitchen shears. Trim away the tough edges of the stem. Rinse each artichoke under cold running water, spreading the leaves to rinse out any residual dirt or sand.

To cook the artichokes, put 3 to 4 inches of water in a deep saucepan large enough to hold all the artichokes snugly so they remain upright as they cook. Stir in the balsamic vinegar, if using. Add the artichokes, making certain they are standing partially upright. Cover and bring to a boil. Cook the artichokes until crisp tender, about 20 minutes. They are done when an outer leaf peels off easily. Remove the artichokes from the pan using tongs and arrange them upside down on a rack set over a large dinner plate to drain and cool. Cover and refrigerate for 4 to 24 hours (see note).

To make the dipping sauce, put the mayonnaise and lemon juice into a small bowl and stir until thoroughly combined. Cover tightly and refrigerate for 2 to 4 hours to allow the flavors to blend.

Just before serving, pull the leaves apart on each artichoke to expose the fuzzy "choke." Scoop out the fuzzy center choke with a grapefruit spoon or teaspoon. Cut off the bottom stem so the artichoke will sit upright on each serving plate.

Arrange each artichoke on a salad-sized plate, then spoon 1 tablespoon of the sauce into each cavity. Garnish with chili powder and Italian seasoning. Serve cold.

CHEF'S NOTE: If you prefer, you may steam the artichokes, rather than boil them. To do so, fit a steamer basket into a deep, medium-sized saucepan with a tight-fitting lid. Add 2 to 3 inches of cold water. Add the artichokes, making certain they are standing partially upright. Cover and bring to a boil. Steam the artichokes until crisp-tender, for about 20 minutes. Proceed with recipe as a directed.

Roasted Butternut Squash with Carrots and Parsnips

MAKES 4 TO 6 SERVINGS

This tasty combo of fall root vegetables makes an appealing side dish whether you're hosting a holiday soirée or a casual weeknight meal.

- 1 medium butternut squash, peeled and cut into ½-inch slices
- 2 tablespoons extra-virgin olive oil, divided
- 2 teaspoons Italian seasoning blend, divided
- ½ teaspoon sea salt, divided, plus more to taste
- 18 to 20 small carrots, peeled and trimmed
- 8 to 10 small parsnips, peeled and trimmed

Preheat the oven to 375 degrees F. Line two large, rimmed baking pans with unbleached parchment paper. Put the butternut squash, 1 tablespoon olive oil, 1 teaspoon Italian seasoning and ¼ teaspoon sea salt into a large bowl and stir to thoroughly combine. Arrange the butternut squash in a single layer on one of the prepared baking sheets.

Put the carrots, parsnips, 1 tablespoon olive oil, 1 teaspoon Italian seasoning and ¼ teaspoon sea salt into a large mixing bowl and stir to combine. Arrange the carrots and parsnips in a single layer on the remaining prepared baking sheet. Put both pans in the oven, and bake for 50 to 70 minutes, or until slightly golden, rotating the vegetables at least once during cooking. Put the pans on a wire rack and let cool for 5 to 10 minutes before serving.

....

Chili-Roasted Sweet Bell Peppers and Onions

MAKES 4 SERVINGS

These delightful roasted peppers and onions are simple to prepare. Leaving the skins on the peppers makes this dish come together quickly and adds texture and nutrition.

- 4 cups seeded and sliced red, orange and/or yellow sweet bell peppers
- 1 medium sweet onion, sliced
- 1 tablespoon extra-virgin olive oil
- 1 teaspoon chili powder

Preheat the oven to 375 degrees F. Line a large, rimmed baking pan with unbleached parchment paper.

Put the sweet peppers, onion, olive oil and chili powder into a medium-sized bowl and toss gently to coat. Transfer the pepper/onion mixture to the prepared baking sheet and arrange in a single layer. Bake for 20 minutes, or until the edges of the peppers and onions are golden and slightly soft. Put the pan on a wire rack and let cool for 10 minutes before serving.

Roasted Sweet Mini Peppers with Fresh Thyme

MAKES 2 TO 3 SERVINGS

Roasting the peppers along with fresh thyme gives a special pop of flavor to this simple dish.

- 1 bag (about 12 ounces) sweet mini peppers
- Leaves from 3 (4-inch) sprigs of fresh thyme (see note)
- 2 teaspoons extra-virgin olive oil
- ⅛ teaspoon sea salt

Preheat the oven to 400 degrees F. Line a large, rimmed baking sheet with unbleached parchment paper.

Slice the peppers in half. Remove the stems and the tiny seeds from the peppers. Put the peppers into a medium-sized bowl, add the thyme leaves, olive oil and sea salt and toss to evenly coat.

Arrange the peppers in a single layer on the prepared sheet. Bake for 15 minutes. Flip the peppers and bake for 10 to 15 minutes, or until the peppers are soft and slightly golden around the edges. Put the pan on a wire rack and let cool for 10 minutes before serving. Serve warm, room temperature, or cover, refrigerate and serve cold.

CHEF'S NOTE: To remove thyme leaves from the stems, place your fingers at the top of the stem and firmly slide the leaves down and off of the woody stem. The leaves will easily slide off of the stem!

Roasted Fennel with Capers and Bread Crumbs

MAKES 4 SERVINGS

Savory, salty, tender and crunchy, this fennel recipe is a winner. Easy to prep for the oven in 10 minutes flat, this dish is the perfect side for any supper, be it casual or elegant. The capers add zing to this Italian veggie staple.

- 1 large bunch fennel, fronds and stalks removed, cut in large chunks
- ½ tablespoon plus 1 teaspoon extra-virgin olive oil, divided
- 2 tablespoons capers, drained
- 2 small slices whole-grain bread
- 1 teaspoon Italian seasoning blend
- ⅛ teaspoon sea salt

Preheat the oven to 400 degrees F. Line a large, rimmed baking sheet with unbleached parchment paper.

Put the fennel chunks and ½ tablespoon olive oil in a large bowl and stir using a large spoon to coat. Arrange the fennel in a single layer on the prepared baking sheet. Top with the capers. Bake for 30 minutes.

Meanwhile, put the bread into a blender and process into coarse crumbs. Put the bread crumbs into a medium-sized bowl and add the Italian seasoning, 1 teaspoon olive oil and salt. Stir with a large spoon to coat the crumbs with the seasonings and oil.

Remove the fennel from the oven. Sprinkle the bread crumb mixture over the fennel in an even layer. Bake for an additional 8 to 12 minutes, or until the fennel is soft and crumbs are golden.

Put the sheet on a wire rack and cool for 10 minutes. Serve warm, or at room temperature.

Roasted Asparagus

MAKES 6 TO 8 SERVINGS

I like to roast asparagus for a quick side dish. Serve this dish for a company meal or a weeknight supper. Served cold, this tasty asparagus makes a lively luncheon salad.

- 2 large bunches asparagus spears, cleaned and trimmed
- 1 tablespoon extra-virgin olive oil
- ½ teaspoon garlic powder
- ½ teaspoon chili powder
- ½ teaspoon sea salt, plus more as needed
- Several grinds of freshly ground black pepper

223

Preheat the oven to 400 degrees F. Line a large, rimmed baking sheet with unbleached parchment paper.

Put the asparagus into a large bowl. Drizzle with the olive oil and sprinkle with the garlic powder, chili powder, sea salt and pepper. Toss gently until the asparagus is evenly coated.

Arrange the asparagus in a single layer on the prepared baking sheet. Bake for 7 to 10 minutes, or until the asparagus is crisp tender, but not mushy. Serve hot or warm, or cover and refrigerate 2 to 24 hours and serve cold.

Garam Masala Sweet Potato Bites

MAKES 4 SERVINGS

A satisfying sweet and spicy surprise awaits when you bite into these dainty and flavorful potato delights.

- 3 large sweet potatoes or yams, peeled and cut into small wedges
- 2 tablespoons maple syrup
- 1 tablespoon garam masala

P reheat the oven to 350 degrees F. Line a large, rimmed baking sheet with unbleached parchment paper.

Put all of the ingredients into a large bowl and stir with a large spoon to combine. Arrange the potatoes in a single layer on the prepared baking sheet. Bake for 50 to 60 minutes, or until golden brown and slightly crisp. Put the pan on a wire rack and let cool for 5 to 10 minutes. Serve immediately.

White Bean and Spinach Sauté

MAKES 2 MAIN DISH SERVINGS OR 4 SIDE DISH SERVINGS

Hearty enough for a light main dish and fancy enough to make a satisfying side, this simple blend of white beans and delicate baby spinach makes a winning combination.

- 1 can (15 to 16 ounces) white beans, drained and rinsed
- 2 cloves garlic, coarsely chopped
- 1 tablespoon extra-virgin olive oil
- ¼ teaspoon crushed red pepper
- 1 pound baby spinach, washed
- 1 to 2 tablespoons water
- 1 teaspoon reduced-sodium tamari

Put the white beans and garlic into a large skillet. Drizzle the olive oil over the top. Cook over medium heat, stirring constantly for 1 minute. Decrease the heat to medium-low and add the crushed red pepper. Cover and cook for 1 minute.

Stir in the spinach and water. Cover and cook for 2 minutes, stirring occasionally. Add the tamari, cover and cook until the spinach has gently wilted and beans are heated through. Serve hot (see note).

CHEF'S NOTE: This dish is delicious served over *Quick Quinoa* (page 237, see variation), *Easy and Flavorful Short Grain Brown Rice* (page 232) or your favorite variety of pasta.

226

JAZZY TIP: If you prefer to use home-cooked beans, use a heaping ½ cup of dried beans, soaked, cooked and drained, in place of one 15 to 16-ounce can of beans. This method may be used in place of any recipe calling for 15 to 16-ounces of canned beans in this book.

Green Beans and Tomatoes

MAKES 3 TO 4 SERVINGS

This vibrant side dish is great to serve when green beans and summer tomatoes are in season. Easy to double or triple, this veggie combo makes a festive companion to a company meal.

- 3 cups trimmed and chopped green beans
- ½ cup diced fresh tomatoes
- 1 tablespoon salted, roasted sunflower seeds
- 1½ teaspoons maple syrup
- 1 teaspoon reduced-sodium tamari
- Freshly ground black pepper, to taste

Fit a steamer basket into a large pot with a tight-fitting lid. Add 2 to 3 inches of cold water, then add the green beans. Cover, bring to a boil and steam for 5 minutes. Add the diced tomatoes and steam for 5 minutes more. Transfer the green beans and tomatoes to a medium-sized bowl. Stir in the sunflower seeds. Top with the maple syrup, tamari and black pepper. Toss well to coat. Serve warm.

Just Like Grandma's Potatoes

MAKES 6 SERVINGS

My grandmother often made a delicious recipe called *Twice Baked Potatoes*. I loved them, but they were packed with cheese, cream and butter. So I have created a flavorful "cheese-like" potato stuffing to replicate Grandma's specialty, but with a rockin' twist.

- 6 large baked potatoes, cooled or cold (see note)
- 5½ tablespoons nondairy milk, divided, plus more as needed
- 2 tablespoons Dijon mustard
- 1½ cups cooked chickpeas (garbanzo beans), drained and rinsed, if canned
- 2 tablespoons plus ½ teaspoon sesame tahini
- ½ teaspoon smoked paprika
- ¼ teaspoon sea salt, plus more to taste
- Several grinds of freshly ground black pepper, to taste
- ¼ teaspoon sweet paprika, plus more for serving
- Chopped fresh parsley, for serving (optional)

P reheat the oven to 375 degrees F. Line the bottom of a 9 by 12-inch or similar sized baking pan with unbleached parchment paper.

Slice each potato in half, lengthwise. Carefully scoop out the pulp, using a teaspoon or grapefruit spoon, leaving about ¼ inch of the potato skin intact. Put the potato pulp into a large bowl.

Add 3 tablespoons nondairy milk and the Dijon mustard to the potato pulp. Mash using a potato masher or large fork until almost smooth.

Put the garbanzo beans, 2½ tablespoons nondairy milk, 2 tablespoons plus ½ teaspoon sesame tahini, smoked paprika, sea salt and several grinds of black pepper into a blender and process until the mixture is smooth.

Add the garbanzo mixture to the potato pulp, and mash until well combined and almost smooth, adding more nondairy milk if the mixture seems dry. Using a large spoon, put one-twelfth of the potato mixture into each potato skin and smooth the top using the back of the spoon or a rubber spatula. Sprinkle the top of each potato half with one-twelfth of the sweet paprika. Arrange the stuffed potato halves in a single layer in the prepared pan.

Cover and bake for 40 to 45 minutes, or until the filling is heated through. Uncover and bake for an additional 5 to 10 minutes, or until the tops of the potatoes are slightly golden and crusty. Cool for 5 to 7 minutes. Serve 2 potato halves, per person, sprinkled with more sweet paprika and optional chopped fresh parsley.

227

CHEF'S NOTE: The potatoes may be baked up to 48 hours in advance of preparing this recipe, and stored (covered) in the refrigerator. To bake the potatoes, carve a small X on the top of each potato to allow steam to escape during baking. Wrap in foil or place the potatoes directly on the center rack of the oven, cut side facing up. Bake at 400 degrees F for about 1 hour, until slightly soft when squeezed (use oven mitts!).

Mini-Cauliflower Bites

MAKES 4 TO 6 SERVINGS

These enticing florets make an excellent side dish for just about any meal. (I have even used them in place of French fries to accompany a vegan burger.) Cauliflower never tasted so good!

- 8 cups large cauliflower florets, or 22 to 24 baby cauliflowers, washed and trimmed
- 3 tablespoons extra-virgin olive oil
- 1 teaspoon ground cumin
- ¾ teaspoon ground turmeric
- ½ teaspoon garlic powder
- ⅛ teaspoon cayenne pepper (see note)
- Several grinds of Himalayan pink salt or sea salt
- 2 teaspoons vegan margarine
- 2 tablespoons freshly squeezed lemon juice

Preheat the oven to 375 degrees F. Line a large, rimmed baking pan with unbleached parchment paper. Put the cauliflower and olive oil into a large bowl and toss with a large spoon or clean hands to coat.

Put the cumin, turmeric, garlic powder, cayenne pepper and salt into a small bowl and stir to combine. Sprinkle the spice mixture over the cauliflower and stir to thoroughly coat the cauliflower. Transfer the cauliflower mixture to the lined pan and arrange in a single layer. Bake for 50 to 60 minutes, or until the cauliflower is soft and has developed a deep brown color around the edges.

Transfer the hot cauliflower to a large bowl and immediately add the margarine. Stir to combine. Pour the lemon juice over the top and stir to combine. Serve warm.

CHEF'S NOTE: For a less spicy version of this recipe, use 1/16 teaspoon cayenne pepper.

Roasted Cauliflower with Red Onion and Sweet Paprika

MAKES 4 TO 6 SERVINGS

Red onion and sweet paprika both dress up this dandy cauliflower dish, while roasting it brings out the flavor of this nutritious, cruciferous vegetable.

- 1 medium head of cauliflower, cut into bite-sized florets
- 1 red onion, thinly sliced
- 1½ tablespoons extra-virgin olive oil
- 2 teaspoons Italian seasoning blend
- 1 teaspoon garlic powder
- 1 teaspoon sweet paprika
- ½ teaspoon ground turmeric
- Sea salt, to taste
- Freshly ground black pepper, to taste

Preheat the oven to 400 degrees F. Line a large, rimmed baking pan with unbleached parchment paper.

Put the cauliflower, onion, olive oil, Italian seasoning, garlic powder, paprika and turmeric into a large bowl and stir with a large spoon to combine. Spread the mixture in a single layer on the lined baking pan. Bake for 45 to 55 minutes, or until the cauliflower is tender but still holds its shape. Season with salt and pepper, to taste.

Red Potato and Cauliflower Mash

MAKES 4 SERVINGS

This is an easy vegetable mash-up to serve as a hearty side dish for any weeknight supper. "Steam-boiling" the cauliflower and spuds makes it easy to mash them right in the pot, saving on clean up time.

- ¾ cup water, plus more as needed
- 3 very large (or 4 medium) red potatoes, cubed
- ½ large head of cauliflower, cut into florets
- 2 cloves garlic, sliced
- 1 teaspoon Italian seasoning blend
- 1 large vegan bouillon cube, crumbled
- 2 teaspoons vegan margarine (optional)

Put all of the ingredients (except the margarine) into a medium-sized saucepan. Cover and bring to a boil over medium heat. Decrease the heat to medium-low and steam/boil the vegetables for 18 to 22 minutes, or until they are very soft, adding more water ¼ cup at a time as needed, making sure to keep the water level at least 1 inch in depth at all times. Move the pot off the heat, and add the optional vegan margarine. Mash the vegetables into a chunky purée using a potato masher (see note). Serve warm.

CHEF'S NOTE: If there appears to be too much cooking water left in the bottom of the steaming pot before mashing the vegetables, carefully skim off some of the liquid so the mash-up does not get "soupy" when serving.

....

Pretty Orange Mash-Up

MAKES 4 SERVINGS

This dish makes a comforting and colorful addition to a festive meal.

- 6 large carrots, peeled and chopped
- 4 yams or sweet potatoes, peeled and chopped
- ¼ cup unsweetened nondairy milk, plus more as needed
- 1 tablespoon vegan margarine, plus more as needed
- 1 teaspoon ground cinnamon
- Sea salt, to taste
- Freshly ground black pepper, to taste

Fit a steamer basket into a large pot with a tight-fitting lid. Add 2 to 3 inches of cold water, then add the carrots and yams. Cover, bring to a boil and steam for about 15 to 20 minutes, until soft but not mushy.

Heat the nondairy milk in a small saucepan over medium-low heat until steaming hot.

Transfer the carrots and yams to a medium-sized bowl. Add the nondairy milk, margarine and cinnamon. Mash with a potato masher or large fork until smooth and lump-free, adding more nondairy milk or margarine as needed to achieve the desired consistency.

Season with salt and pepper, to taste. Serve immediately.

Russet Oven Fries

MAKES 4 SERVINGS

Who doesn't love thick and crispy steak-style fries? This tasty version is baked in the oven, making it lower in fat than the classic fried potato. So get the catsup and dig in!

- 8 small russet potatoes, scrubbed and cut into small wedges
- 1 tablespoon extra-virgin olive oil
- 2 teaspoons all-purpose seasoning
- ½ teaspoon sweet paprika
- Several grinds of freshly ground black pepper
- ¼ teaspoon sea salt, plus more to taste

Preheat the oven to 375 degrees F. Line a large, rimmed baking sheet with unbleached parchment paper.

Put the potato wedges, olive oil, all-purpose seasoning, paprika and freshly ground pepper into a large bowl and stir with a large spoon until well coated.

Arrange the potato wedges in a single layer on the prepared baking sheet. Bake for 30 minutes. Remove from the oven, flip the potatoes and sprinkle with ¼ teaspoon sea salt. Bake for an additional 20 to 30 minutes or until nicely golden around the edges. Put the pan on a wire rack and let cool for 10 minutes. Season with more sea salt, to taste. Serve immediately.

Easy and Flavorful Short Grain Brown Rice

MAKES (ABOUT) 3 CUPS

Short grain brown rice has a nutty taste that makes a satisfying side dish for many plant-based meals. Make a double batch to have on hand for adding to soups, stews, stir-fries, salads and so much more.

- 2 cups water, plus more as needed
- 1 cup short grain brown rice
- ½ large vegan bouillon cube, crumbled

Put all of the ingredients into a medium-sized saucepan. Cover and bring to a boil over medium-high heat. Decrease the heat to low and simmer for 40 to 50 minutes, or until the rice is tender and all of the water is absorbed (see note).

Remove the rice from heat, uncover and gently fluff with a fork. Cover and let stand 10 to 12 minutes before serving. Stored tightly covered in the refrigerator, the rice will keep up to 4 days.

CHEF'S NOTE: If all of the water becomes absorbed, and the rice is not yet tender, add an additional 2 tablespoons of water.

Spicy Rice

MAKES 6 SERVINGS

The perfect complement to any savory meal, this rice has just the right amount of spicy flavor to serve with a stew, steamed vegetables or just about any entrée.

- 4½ cups water

- 2 cups brown basmati rice

- 1 teaspoon *Jazzy Sazón* (page 81)

Put all of the ingredients into a medium-sized saucepan. Cover and bring to a boil over medium-high heat. Decrease the heat to low and simmer for 40 to 45 minutes or until almost all of the water is absorbed. Remove the rice from heat, uncover and gently fluff with a fork. Cover and let stand for 10 to 12 minutes before serving. Stored tightly covered in the refrigerator, the rice will keep up to 4 days.

Colorful Confetti Fries

MAKES 4 SERVINGS

This tantalizing mix of russet potatoes and sweet potatoes is delicious. Tossing them with a bit of olive oil and then baking them in the oven turns these spuds into tasty "fries!" They are perfect to serve with *Sunny Black Bean Burgers* (page 194).

- 2 large russet potatoes, scrubbed
- 2 large sweet potatoes or yams, scrubbed
- 1 tablespoon extra-virgin olive oil, plus more as needed
- 1 teaspoon Italian seasoning blend
- ¾ teaspoon chili powder
- ¾ teaspoon garlic powder
- ½ teaspoon sea salt, plus more as needed
- Freshly ground black pepper, to taste (optional)

Preheat the oven to 400 degrees F. Line a large, rimmed baking sheet with parchment paper.

Cut the potatoes into matchsticks. Put the potatoes, olive oil, Italian seasoning, chili powder and garlic powder into a large bowl and gently toss with clean hands or a large spoon, until the potatoes are evenly coated.

Arrange the potatoes in a single layer on the lined baking sheet. Bake for 25 minutes and remove from the oven. Sprinkle with salt and gently stir to coat. Bake for an additional 15 to 20 minutes or until the potatoes are soft inside and golden on the outside. Taste and add more sea salt and the optional black pepper, to taste. Serve immediately with *Quick Catsup-Mayo Sauce* or *Quick Marinara-Mayo Sauce* (page 75) on the side.

Festive Quinoa with Cranberries

MAKES 3 TO 4 SERVINGS

This holiday side dish features quinoa, which is considered to be a complete protein source, making it the perfect addition to any celebratory meal. The cranberries give it a slight tang and a pretty pop of color. This easy and fast cooking recipe makes an ideal alternative to rice or potatoes, while scoring high on taste and nutrition.

- 2 cups water

- 1 cup quinoa, rinsed thoroughly

- 3 tablespoons sweetened dried cranberries (see note)

- 1 teaspoon vegan margarine

- ⅛ teaspoon sea salt, plus more as needed

CHEF'S NOTE: You may use dried cherries in place of the cranberries in this recipe.

Put the water, quinoa, cranberries, margarine and salt into a medium-sized saucepan and bring to a boil over medium-high heat. Decrease the heat to medium-low, cover and cook for 15 to 17 minutes or until the water is absorbed. Remove the quinoa from heat, uncover and gently fluff with a fork. Cover and let stand for 5 to 7 minutes before serving. Stored tightly covered in the refrigerator, the quinoa and cranberries will keep up to 2 days.

236

Turmeric Quinoa

MAKES 3 TO 4 SERVINGS

This is a festive and delicious way to serve quinoa. Try making a double batch to have on hand for stuffing mushrooms, zucchini or peppers, or for using in casseroles, soups and salads.

- •1 cup quinoa, rinsed thoroughly
- •2 cups water
- •½ teaspoon ground turmeric
- •½ large vegan bouillon cube, crumbled (see note)

Put all of the ingredients into a medium-sized saucepan. Cover and bring to a simmer over medium-high heat. Decrease the heat to medium-low, cover and cook for 15 to 17 minutes, or until all of the water is absorbed. Remove the quinoa from heat, uncover and gently fluff with a fork. Cover and let stand for 5 to 7 minutes before serving. Stored tightly covered in the refrigerator, the quinoa will keep up to 3 days.

CHEF'S NOTE: If desired, you may use 2 cups of prepared vegetable broth in place of the water and bouillon cube.

VARIATION: Basic (Quick) Quinoa – Omit the turmeric. Proceed with recipe as directed for a simple and nutritious side dish to pair with any meal.

CHAPTER THIRTEEN
Cakes, Crumbles, Cookies and Crisps

The sweets in this chapter are sure to please kids and adults alike! From fruit crisps and crumbles to festive and fun cookies and cakes, let's celebrate with these scrumptious vegan versions of classic treats.

Recipes

Divine Chocolate Mousse Cake

MAKES 8 TO 10 SERVINGS

This delectable little chocolate cake is so delicious, you will have folks asking for more, more, more! If you do not already have 6-inch round cake pans, I highly recommend adding them to your baking equipment, as they are very handy for making a variety of petite cakes.

MOUSSE FROSTING

- ¾ cup chocolate flavored nondairy milk (I like cashew milk for this)
- 1 block (14 to 16 ounces) extra-firm regular tofu, drained
- 1 tablespoon extra-virgin olive oil
- 1 teaspoon vanilla extract
- 3 tablespoons vegan powdered sugar
- 1 cup (55% cacao) vegan dark chocolate chips, plus 30 to 35 more for decorating the cake

CAKE

- 1 tablespoon flaxseeds
- 1 cup plus 2 tablespoons whole wheat flour
- ⅔ cup vegan cane sugar
- 3 tablespoons unsweetened cocoa powder
- ¾ teaspoon baking soda
- ⅛ teaspoon sea salt
- ¾ cup plus 3½ tablespoons nondairy milk
- 2½ tablespoons "extra-light" olive oil (see note)
- ½ teaspoon vanilla extract

FILLING

- 3 heaping tablespoons raspberry preserves, plus more as needed

To make the frosting, heat the nondairy milk in a small saucepan over medium-low heat until small bubbles appear on the surface and the nondairy milk is simmering hot.

Put the tofu, olive oil, vanilla extract and powdered sugar into a blender, then add 1 cup of chocolate chips. Pour in the simmering nondairy milk and immediately process for 30 seconds to 1 minute, or until *completely* smooth. Spoon the mixture into a small bowl, cover and refrigerate until completely chilled (about 3 to 4 hours) before frosting your cake.

To make the cake, preheat the oven to 350 degrees F. Liberally coat three 6-inch round cake pans with vegan margarine. (If you are not using nonstick cake pans, line the bottom of each pan with parchment paper and liberally coat the parchment paper with vegan margarine.)

Put the flaxseeds into a high-performance blending appliance and process into fine flour. Put the flaxseed flour, whole wheat flour, cane sugar, cocoa powder, baking soda and sea salt into a large bowl and stir with a dry whisk to combine. Add the nondairy milk, olive oil and vanilla and stir with a large spoon to incorporate. Divide the cake evenly among the three prepared cake pans. Bake for 16 to 20 minutes or until a toothpick inserted into the center of each cake comes out clean. Put the cake pans on wire racks, and run a table knife around the perimeter of each cake to loosen the sides. Let cool for 15 minutes. Turn the cakes out onto the wire racks. (If you are using parchment paper, gently and *very carefully* remove the parchment paper.) Let cool for at least 2 hours before frosting the cakes.

To frost the cakes, line the perimeter of a pretty plate with strips of parchment paper. Put one cake layer in the center of the plate. Spoon half of the raspberry preserves over the first cake layer and spread in an even layer using an offset spatula. Spoon about one-quarter of the frosting over the raspberry preserves and *gently* spread it in an even layer, over the preserves, using the spatula. The frosting layer will be *very* thick.

Put the second cake layer on the frosting and gently press down, so the cake will adhere. Spoon the remaining half of the raspberry preserves over the second cake layer and spread in an even layer using an offset spatula. Spoon about one-quarter of the frosting over the raspberry preserves and *gently* spread it in a thick, even layer over the preserves, using the spatula.

Position the third cake layer on the frosting and gently press down, so the cake will adhere. Spoon the remaining frosting over the top and sides of the cake and gently spread it evenly over the top and sides, using an offset spatula (once again, the frosting layer will be *very* thick). Decorate in a pleasing manner with the reserved chocolate chips.

Refrigerate for at least 2 hours and make certain to serve the cake *well-chilled*. Covered and stored in the refrigerator, the cake will keep for 3 days. (It actually tastes better the longer it stands in the refrigerator!)

CHEF'S NOTE: If desired, you may use extra-virgin olive oil in place of the light olive oil, but the cake will be slightly denser in texture.

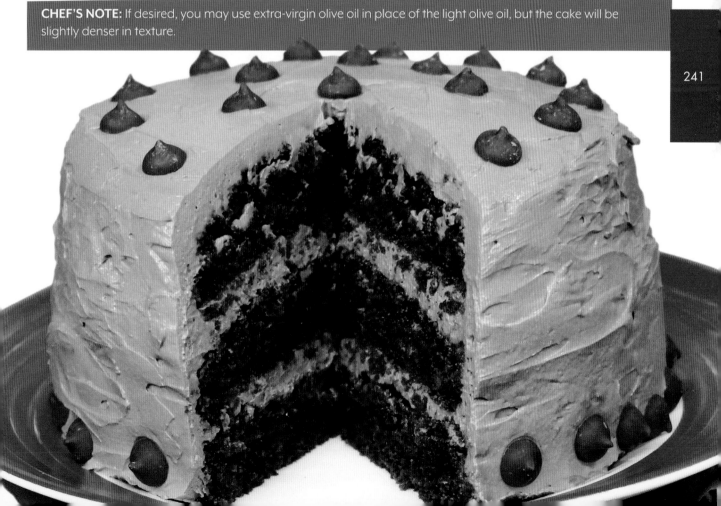

Clementine-Cranberry Cake

**MAKES TWO 6-INCH CAKES
(10 TO 12 SERVINGS)**

GLAZE

- 3 tablespoons clementine juice (from about 1 clementine)
- 3 tablespoons vegan powdered sugar

CAKE

- 1½ cups whole wheat pastry flour, plus more for coating pan
- 1 teaspoon baking powder
- ½ teaspoon baking soda
- ¼ teaspoon sea salt
- ⅔ cup vegan cane sugar
- ½ cup plus 1 tablespoon clementine juice (from 3 to 5 clementines)
- ½ cup vanilla flavored nondairy milk
- ¼ cup extra-virgin olive oil
- 1 teaspoon vanilla extract
- ⅔ cup fresh cranberries

GARNISH

- 2 clementines, peeled and divided into individual sections

This delightfully delicious and *almost* decadent cake makes a fabulous finish to a merry meal. Tart cranberries, juxtaposed with seasonal sweet clementines, provide a surprising combination that makes a dazzling dessert.

Preheat the oven to 375 degrees F. Lightly coat two 6-inch round baking pans with vegan margarine and lightly flour them.

For the glaze, put 3 tablespoons clementine juice and 3 tablespoons powdered sugar into a small bowl. Whisk briskly to combine. Cover and refrigerate for 1 hour, while preparing the cake.

To make the cakes, put the pastry flour, baking powder, baking soda and sea salt into a large bowl and stir with a dry whisk to combine. Whisk in the sugar. Add ½ cup plus 1 tablespoon clementine juice, nondairy milk, olive oil and vanilla extract, and stir with a large spoon to incorporate. Fold in the cranberries.

Divide the batter evenly between the two prepared cake pans. Bake for 23 to 27 minutes, or until a toothpick inserted into the center of each cake comes out clean.

Put the pans on a wire rack and loosen the sides of each cake with a knife. Let cool 5 minutes.

Using a toothpick, poke about 10 holes into the top of each cake. Let cool 5 to 10 minutes more and gently turn each cake out of the pan. Flip the cakes (hole side up) and put on the wire rack. Carefully pour half of the glaze over each cake. Let cool 15 minutes.

Garnish with clementine sections and serve warm. Alternately, let the cakes cool completely and serve at room temperature, or loosely cover the cakes and refrigerate for 4 hours (or overnight) and serve chilled. Stored covered in the refrigerator, leftover cake will keep 1 day.

Coconut, Orange and Carrot Mini-Cakes

**MAKES THREE 6-INCH CAKES
(12 TO 14 SERVINGS)**

These rich and moist cakes are as tasty as they are cute. Orange juice stands in for milk and flaxseeds make an excellent substitute for the oil and eggs. Topped with a decadent vegan cream cheese frosting, this dessert is a real standout.

VEGAN CREAM CHEESE FROSTING

- 2 containers (8 ounces each) vegan cream cheese
- ¼ cup vegan margarine
- 2 teaspoons vanilla extract
- 1 cup plus 2 tablespoons vegan confectioner's (powdered) sugar

....

CAKE

- 2 cups whole wheat flour
- 1½ teaspoons baking powder
- ½ teaspoon baking soda
- 2 tablespoons freshly ground golden flaxseeds
- ⅓ cup unsweetened shredded dried coconut
- ¾ cup firmly packed vegan dark brown sugar
- 1¼ cups freshly squeezed orange juice (zest the oranges first)
- ⅔ cup water
- 1 tablespoon vanilla extract
- 1⅓ cups plus 2 tablespoons peeled and shredded carrots
- ½ cup raisins
- 2 tablespoons orange zest

P reheat the oven to 350 degrees F. Lightly coat three 6-inch round cake pans with vegan margarine.

To make the frosting, put the vegan cream cheese, margarine and vanilla extract into a small bowl and stir briskly with a fork until smooth and thoroughly combined. Stir in the vegan powdered sugar and mix until incorporated and smooth. Cover and refrigerate for 3 to 4 hours before using.

To make the cake, put the whole wheat flour, baking powder and baking soda into a large bowl and stir with a dry whisk to combine. Add the ground flaxseeds, coconut and brown sugar and stir with the whisk to combine.

Stir the orange juice, water and vanilla into the flour mixture and mix with a large spoon just until incorporated. Add 1⅓ cups of the shredded carrots, raisins and 1 tablespoon orange zest and mix until incorporated.

Pour one-third of the batter into each of the prepared cake pans. Bake 33 to 37 minutes, or until a toothpick inserted into the center of each cake comes out clean.

Put the pans on a wire rack and gently loosen the sides of the cakes with a knife. Cool for 5 to 7 minutes and carefully invert each cake onto the rack. Let cool *completely* (about 2 hours) before frosting the cakes.

To keep your serving plates from getting covered with frosting, arrange unbleached parchment paper strips around the edge of three pretty plates. Put 1 of the cakes on a prepared plate. Spread one-third of the frosting over the top and sides of the first cake, using an offset spatula or table knife. Gently pull the parchment paper strips from the cake. Repeat with the remaining two cakes (alternately, you may pipe the frosting onto the cakes, using a large star tip). (See note).

Cover and refrigerate for at least 2 hours, or up to 24 hours before serving. To serve, cut a slice of cake and put it on a dessert plate, garnished with a bit of the remaining shredded carrots and orange zest. Covered tightly and stored in the refrigerator, leftover cakes will keep for about 3 days.

CHEF'S NOTE: For a lighter cake, omit the frosting and dust each cake liberally with 1 to 2 tablespoons of vegan powdered sugar.

Blueberry Tea Cakes with Vegan Lemon "Buttercream" Glaze

MAKES 12 CAKES

These delectable little cakes make a fantastic finish to any spring or summer meal. Showcasing fresh plump blueberries, these delicate cakes are then drizzled with a luscious lemon glaze. These mini-cakes will really impress family and guests alike. Oh yes, did I mention? Sans the glaze, they make tasty breakfast muffins or a satisfying sweet snack.

GLAZE

- ⅓ cup vegan margarine
- 1½ tablespoons freshly squeezed lemon juice
- 2 cups vegan powdered sugar, divided, plus more if needed
- 2 tablespoons nondairy milk

CAKES

- 1 cup sweetened nondairy milk
- 2 tablespoons freshly squeezed lemon juice
- 1¼ cups whole wheat flour, plus more for coating pan
- 1¼ teaspoons baking powder
- ¼ teaspoon baking soda
- 1 teaspoon ground cinnamon
- ¾ cup vegan cane sugar
- 2 tablespoons extra-virgin olive oil
- ½ cup water
- 2½ cups fresh blueberries

To prepare the glaze, put the margarine and 1½ tablespoons of lemon juice into a medium-sized bowl and stir vigorously with a fork to combine. Add 1 cup of the powdered sugar and briskly stir with the fork until all of the sugar is incorporated. Add the second cup of powdered sugar and 2 tablespoons nondairy milk and stir until the glaze is nice and smooth. Cover and refrigerate for about 2 hours to allow the glaze to thicken slightly.

To make the cakes, preheat the oven to 350 degrees F. Put the nondairy milk and lemon juice into a small bowl or pitcher and stir to combine. Let stand for 10 minutes while preparing the batter.

Generously coat two 6-cup jumbo muffin tins with vegan margarine. Sprinkle a bit of the flour into the bottom of each muffin cup and tilt the pan, tapping to move the flour evenly around the insides of the muffin cups, until each cup is coated with a very thin film of flour. Tap out any extra flour. Put 1¼ cups flour, baking powder, baking soda and cinnamon into a large bowl and stir with a dry whisk until combined. Add the sugar and stir with a whisk to combine.

247

Add the oil to the nondairy milk/lemon mixture, and stir vigorously with a whisk or fork to combine. Add the water and the nondairy milk/lemon mixture to the flour mixture and stir with a large spoon, until well moistened, to make a batter. Gently fold the blueberries into the batter and stir to combine.

Divide the batter among the muffin cups. Bake for 30 minutes, or until a toothpick inserted into the center of a tea cake comes out clean.

Put the tins on a wire rack and loosen the edges of the cakes with a knife. Let cool for 5 to 7 minutes. Carefully invert the tins onto a wire rack and gently shake to loosen the cakes. Cakes will be very, very soft, so carefully arrange them on the wire rack to firm up a bit and thoroughly cool (about 2 hours).

Once the cakes have cooled, drizzle one-twelfth of the glaze over each cake. Refrigerate for at least 2 hours, or up to 6 hours before serving. Let the cakes stand at room temperature for about 20 minutes before serving. Tightly covered and stored in the refrigerator, the cakes will keep for about 2 days.

Blueberry Tea Cakes (without glaze, page 246)

Lively Lemony Cupcakes

MAKES 12 CUPCAKES

Part cupcake, part muffin, these lively cakes are moist and sweet, laced with a tangy lemon taste. For convenience, I sometimes use a ready-made vegan frosting (as I have here), but if you have extra time you can top these tasty treats with *Vanilla Dessert Topping* (page 78), *Vegan Cream Cheese Frosting* (page 244), *Tofu-Cashew Whipped Cream* (page 78) or your favorite homemade frosting.

CUPCAKES

- 1¼ cups nondairy milk
- ⅓ cup freshly squeezed lemon juice (from about 2 large lemons; zest the lemons first, before squeezing)
- 2⅓ cups whole wheat flour, plus more as needed
- 1½ teaspoons baking powder
- ½ teaspoon baking soda
- 1 cup vegan cane sugar
- ¼ cup water, plus more as needed
- 2 tablespoons extra-light olive oil (see note)
- Lemon zest from 2 large lemons

FROSTING

- 1 to 1½ containers (12 to 18 ounces) ready-made vegan vanilla frosting, or your favorite homemade frosting

Preheat the oven to 375 degrees F. Line a 12-cup standard muffin tin with paper liners.

Put the nondairy milk and lemon juice into a bowl or pitcher and stir to combine. Let the mixture stand for 7 to 10 minutes, while preparing the rest of the cupcake batter. (It will curdle to make "vegan buttermilk.")

Put the flour, baking powder and baking soda into a large bowl and stir with a dry whisk to combine. Add the sugar and stir with the whisk to combine. Stir in the water, olive oil and the "vegan buttermilk." Fold in 1½ teaspoons of the lemon zest.

If the batter seems overly wet, stir in a bit more flour, 1 tablespoon at a time, until the mixture is moist but not runny. Alternately, if the batter seems overly dry, stir in a bit more water, 1 tablespoon at a time, until the mixture is moist.

Mound the mixture into the lined cups. Bake for 25 minutes, or until set and a toothpick inserted in the middle of a cupcake comes out clean. Put the tin on a wire rack. Let cool for 10 minutes, then remove the cupcakes and put on a wire rack. Cool the cupcakes completely (at least 1 hour) before frosting them.

Spoon the frosting into a piping bag that has been fitted with a star tip. Pipe a generous amount of frosting on top of each cupcake. (Alternately, spoon some frosting or whipped topping on top of each cupcake and spread in an even layer with an offset spatula). Garnish each cupcake with some of the remaining lemon zest.

Serve immediately, or put the cupcakes into a tightly covered container and refrigerate. For best taste, remove the cupcakes from the refrigerator about 15 minutes before serving.

CHEF'S NOTE: If desired, you may use extra-virgin olive oil in place of the light olive oil, but the cupcakes will be slightly denser in texture.

Mini Raspberry Cheeze-Cakes

MAKES 12 MINI-CAKES

Delicate and delightful, but not too sweet, these *cheezy* cakes showcase fresh raspberries nestled in a tofu cheese-like filling, with a gluten-free, flourless fruit and nut crust. So good.

CRUST

- ½ cup raisins
- ½ cup chopped pecans
- ½ cup unsweetened shredded dried coconut

FILLING

- 1 block (14 to 16 ounces) extra-firm regular tofu, well drained
- 1 aseptic box (12 to 12½ ounces) firm silken tofu, well drained
- 3 tablespoons maple syrup
- 1 teaspoon vanilla extract

TOPPING

- 5 teaspoons maple syrup, divided
- ⅓ cup apricot preserves
- 2 teaspoons water
- 36 fresh raspberries

Preheat the oven to 350 degrees F. Thoroughly coat a 12-cup standard muffin tin with vegan margarine.

To make the crust, put the raisins, pecans and coconut into a high-performance blending appliance and process until the mixture forms soft dough. Transfer the dough to a plate. Put 1 heaping tablespoon of the dough into each of the prepared muffin cups and gently press it into the bottom of the cup to make a crust. Continue in this manner to make 12 crusts. Pre-bake the crusts for 6 minutes. Put the tin on a wire rack and let cool for 10 to 15 minutes before adding the filling.

Once the crusts have cooled, put the filling ingredients into a high-performance blending appliance and process until very smooth. Divide the filling evenly among the 12 muffin cups, smoothing out the top as you go. Bake for 24 to 26 minutes, or until the filling is almost set. Put the pan on a wire rack and loosen the sides of each mini-cake with a knife. Drizzle ¼ teaspoon of maple syrup over the top of each mini-cake. Let cool 10 minutes, then *carefully* remove each mini-cake from the muffin cup, and place it on the wire rack to cool for 15 minutes.

While the mini-cakes cool, put ⅓ cup apricot preserves, the remaining 2 teaspoons maple syrup and 2 teaspoons of water into a small bowl and briskly whisk until combined. Spoon about 1½ heaping teaspoons of the mixture over the top of each mini-cake. Artfully press 3 raspberries into the top of each mini-cake. Refrigerate at least 4 hours before serving. Loosely covered and stored in the refrigerator, the mini-cakes will keep for 1 day.

Better Than Apple Pie

MAKES 6 TO 8 SERVINGS

Last Thanksgiving I decided to get creative with my dessert. Rather than preparing a classic apple pie, I whipped up a fantastic crisp with a base of apples, pears and dried cranberries to give it a festive holiday twist. Topped with oats, sunflower seeds and coconut, the topping stands in beautifully for a traditional crust. After serving my twist on a much-loved holiday treat, my sister exclaimed, "Wow! This is *better* than apple pie!" Enough said.

FILLING

- 4 medium Bosc or D'Anjou pears, cored and sliced (do not peel)
- 3 medium sweet red apples, cored and sliced (do not peel)
- ½ cup sweetened dried cranberries
- 2 tablespoons freshly squeezed lemon juice
- ½ cup firmly packed dark brown sugar
- 2½ tablespoons maple syrup (see note)
- 2 teaspoons ground cinnamon

TOPPING

- 2 cups rolled oats
- ½ cup raw, unsalted sunflower seeds
- ⅓ cup plus 2 tablespoons firmly packed dark brown sugar
- ⅓ cup unsweetened shredded dried coconut
- 1 teaspoon ground cinnamon
- ⅓ cup vegan margarine, softened
- 2 tablespoons maple syrup

Preheat the oven to 350 degrees F. Liberally coat a 9 by 12-inch or similar sized casserole dish with vegan margarine.

To make the filling, put the pears, apples, cranberries and lemon juice into a medium-sized bowl and gently toss with a large spoon to combine. Add ½ cup brown sugar, 2½ tablespoons maple syrup and 2 teaspoons cinnamon and stir with a large spoon to coat. Transfer the fruit mixture to the prepared dish.

To make the topping, put the oats, sunflower seeds, ⅓ cup plus 2 tablespoons brown sugar, coconut and 1 teaspoon cinnamon into a medium-sized bowl and stir with a large spoon to combine. Add the vegan margarine and mix it into the oat mixture until thoroughly combined, using your hands or a dough blender.

Spread the oat mixture in an even layer over the fruit and drizzle 2 tablespoons of maple syrup evenly over the top. Cover and bake for 35 to 40 minutes, or until the fruit begins to soften. Uncover and bake for an additional 10 to 12 minutes, or until the topping is crisp and the fruit filling is bubbling hot. Put the dish on a wire rack and let cool for at least 20 minutes before serving. Serve warm or at room temperature, or cover and refrigerate for 3 to 4 hours and serve cold. The crisp is delicious served with vanilla flavored vegan "ice cream," *Vanilla Dessert Topping* (page 78) or *Tofu-Cashew Whipped Cream* (page 78) on the side. Tightly covered and stored in the refrigerator, the "pie" will keep for up to 3 days.

CHEF'S NOTE: For a less sweet dessert, omit the 2½ tablespoons maple syrup in the filling. Proceed with recipe as directed.

255

Raspberry-Coconut Apple Crisp

MAKES 6 SERVINGS

The crispy topping combined with a sweet fruit filling makes a luscious dessert, afternoon snack or delightful breakfast treat. This recipe makes great use of seasonal fall apples, and you can use any variety of apples that you have on hand or prefer.

FILLING

- 3 medium to large apples, cored and cubed (do not peel)
- 3 tablespoons raspberry preserves
- 1 teaspoon ground cinnamon
- 1 teaspoon vanilla extract

....

TOPPING

- 1 cup rolled oats
- ⅓ cup plus 1 tablespoon chopped pecans
- ⅓ cup unsweetened shredded dried coconut
- ¼ cup plus 2 tablespoons lightly packed dark brown sugar
- ¼ cup toasted wheat germ or oat bran
- ¼ cup vegan margarine

Preheat the oven to 350 degrees F. Put the apples, preserves, cinnamon and vanilla into a medium-sized bowl and stir to combine. Transfer the mixture to a 9 by 12-inch or similar sized casserole dish.

Put all of the topping ingredients into a medium-sized bowl and combine using a dough blender or large fork until the vegan margarine is incorporated. Spread the topping mixture evenly over the apple/raspberry mixture. Cover and bake for 35 to 40 minutes or until the apples begin to soften. Uncover and bake for an additional 10 to 12 minutes, or until the topping is crisp and filling is bubbling hot. Put the dish on a wire rack and let cool at least 30 minutes before serving. Store leftover crisp, tightly covered in the refrigerator, for up to 2 days.

Apple, Banana and Cranberry Crumble

MAKES 4 SERVINGS

This delightful crumble is oil-free, quick-to-prep, satisfying and truly delicious. It serves double duty as a healthful dessert or sweet afternoon snack!

APPLE LAYER

- 4 medium tart green apples, cored and sliced (do not peel)
- 4 tablespoons sweetened dried cranberries
- 2 tablespoons maple syrup
- 1 teaspoon ground cinnamon

OAT LAYER

- 1 medium ripe banana
- 1 tablespoon maple syrup
- 1 rounded teaspoon ground cinnamon
- 1¼ cups rolled oats

Preheat the oven to 350 degrees F.

Put the apples in a medium-sized bowl. Add the cranberries, 2 tablespoons maple syrup and 1 teaspoon ground cinnamon. Stir the mixture with a large spoon to coat. Transfer to a 9 by 12-inch or similar sized casserole.

Put the banana, 1 tablespoon maple syrup and 1 rounded teaspoon ground cinnamon into a medium-sized bowl. Mash together using a potato masher or large fork until almost smooth, allowing a few small chunks to remain. Add the rolled oats and mix with a large spoon to combine. Spread the banana/oat mixture over the apples in an even layer.

Cover and bake for 35 to 40 minutes or until the apples are soft. Uncover and bake for an additional 5 minutes, or until the topping is slightly crisp.

Transfer the casserole to a wire rack, and let cool 5 minutes before serving. Tightly covered and stored in the refrigerator, the crisp will keep for 1 day.

Chocolate-Banana Gratin

MAKES 3 SERVINGS

Sugary-tasting and satisfying, this enticing bread pudding makes a delicious dessert or fun breakfast option. Sliced bananas and dried cranberries drenched in chocolate nondairy milk and a bit of maple syrup plump up as they bake for a sweet surprise!

- 3 slices whole-grain bread, cubed
- 3 medium bananas, sliced
- ⅓ cup sweetened dried cranberries
- 1 cup chocolate flavored nondairy milk
- 2 tablespoons maple syrup
- 1 teaspoon vanilla extract

Preheat the oven to 375 degrees F. Liberally coat an 11 by 8-inch or similar sized baking dish with vegan margarine.

Put the bread, bananas and cranberries into a medium-sized bowl and gently stir with a large spoon to combine. Put the nondairy milk, maple syrup and vanilla into a small bowl and whisk to combine. Pour the nondairy milk mixture over the bread mixture and gently stir to coat. Let stand 2 minutes.

Transfer the bread mixture to the prepared dish and spread in an even layer. Bake, uncovered, for 25 to 35 minutes, or until hot and bubbling and the top of the pudding is a bit golden. Put the dish on a wire rack and let cool 7 to 10 minutes before serving. Serve alone, or with *Tofu-Cashew Whipped Cream* (page 78) or *Vanilla Dessert Topping* (page 78) on the side. Stored in a tightly covered container in the refrigerator, leftover gratin will keep for 1 day.

Blueberry-Cranberry Cookies

MAKES 14 TO 16 COOKIES

Six ingredients and six minutes is all it takes to assemble these tasty cookies for the oven. Perfect for an afternoon snack, late night dessert or even an "on-the-go" breakfast, you'll find these dashing dainties are an excellent addition to your sweet treats recipes.

- 2 medium ripe bananas

- 1 teaspoon vanilla extract

- 1 cup rolled oats

- ¼ cup shredded unsweetened dried coconut

- ¼ cup sweetened dried cranberries

- 2½ to 3 heaping tablespoons blueberry preserves, plus more as needed

Preheat the oven to 350 degrees F. Line a large, rimmed baking sheet with unbleached parchment paper.

Put the banana and the vanilla extract into a large bowl and mash using a potato masher or large fork until almost smooth. Some chunks should remain.

Add the oats and coconut to the banana mixture and stir with a large spoon to combine. Fold in the cranberries. Scoop up a heaping tablespoon of the dough and place it on the lined pan. Flatten slightly with a flat spatula. Using your thumb or index finger (or the back of a small spoon), make a little well in the center of the cookie. Continue in this manner with the remaining cookie dough.

Put the preserves into a small bowl. Fill each cookie with a heaping ½ teaspoon of the blueberry preserves.

Bake for 12 to 16 minutes, or until the underside of the cookies are very golden and the edges are slightly golden in color. Put the pan on a wire rack and let the cookies cool for 2 minutes. Carefully transfer the cookies directly to the wire rack and let them cool at least 15 minutes before serving. Stored in an airtight container in the refrigerator, the cookies will keep for about 2 days.

VARIATION: Raspberry-Raisin Cookies - Substitute raspberry preserves for the blueberry preserves, and substitute raisins for the cranberries. Proceed with the recipe as directed.

CHAPTER FOURTEEN
Pies, Puddings, Tarts and Treats

An amazing dessert can make a meal, and these fanciful treats will surely add pizzazz to any festive meal. Featuring a classic southern pie, a rich and decadent pudding and a tart fit for royalty, these vegan sweets will round out your menu with a scrumptious flair.

Recipes

Royal Apple Tart

MAKES 6 SERVINGS

Fit for a king or queen, this beautiful tart showcases tender apple slices displayed on a moist, flourless crust. Healthy and nutritious (but totally delicious), this stunning dessert will impress your family and guests alike. The long list of ingredients and additional effort needed to prepare this delicacy is well worth the delicious results.

APPLE TOPPING

- 3 large apples (any variety), peeled, cored and cut into ½ inch slices
- 1 tablespoon maple syrup
- 2 teaspoons ground cinnamon
- 2 teaspoons vanilla extract

CRUST

- 2 medium ripe bananas
- 1 tablespoon maple syrup
- 1 teaspoon vanilla extract
- 1 teaspoon ground cinnamon
- 1 cup rolled oats
- ½ cup shredded unsweetened dried coconut
- 3 tablespoons toasted wheat germ (see note)
- ¼ cup sweetened dried cranberries (see note)

GLAZE

- 1 tablespoon maple syrup
- ⅓ cup raspberry preserves
- 4 to 5 teaspoons water
- 1 tablespoon vegan cane sugar

Preheat the oven to 350 degrees F. Lightly coat a 9-inch round springform pan with vegan margarine. Line a rimmed baking sheet large enough to accommodate the springform pan with unbleached parchment paper.

To make the topping, put the apples, 1 tablespoon maple syrup, 2 teaspoons cinnamon and 2 teaspoons vanilla into a medium-sized bowl and stir to thoroughly coat. Let stand, while preparing the crust.

To make the crust, put the bananas, 1 tablespoon maple syrup, 1 teaspoon vanilla and 1 teaspoon cinnamon into a medium-sized bowl, and mash using a potato masher or large fork until almost smooth, but a few chunks still remain. Add the oats, coconut and wheat germ and stir with a large spoon to thoroughly combine. Fold in the cranberries. Press the crust into the prepared pan, using the bottom of a measuring cup.

Artfully arrange the apple slices in a spiral fashion over the top of the crust. Spread 1 tablespoon maple syrup over the apple slices, using a pastry brush or teaspoon. Bake for 30 minutes.

Meanwhile, put the raspberry preserves and water into a small bowl and briskly whisk to combine. Remove the tart from the oven and spread the raspberry preserve mixture over the top of the apples, using a small pastry brush or teaspoon. Put the tart on the parchment-lined baking sheet (this will protect your oven from preserves that may drip from the springform pan as the tart bakes). Tent the tart with foil and bake for an additional 15 to 25 minutes, or until the apples are soft and the top is slightly golden.

Remove the tart from the oven and sprinkle the cane sugar over the top of the apples. Bake for 1 to 3 minutes, or until the top is slightly golden. Put the pan on a wire rack. Carefully run a table knife around the perimeter of the tart, to ensure it does not stick to the side of the pan. Let the tart cool for 10 minutes and then remove the side of the springform pan.

Let the tart cool for at least 20 minutes more before serving. Serve warm with vegan ice cream or *Vanilla Dessert Topping* (page 78) on the side, or cover, refrigerate for 4 to 6 hours and serve cold. Stored covered in the refrigerator, the tart will keep for 2 days.

CHEF'S NOTES:
- You may use toasted oat bran in place of the wheat germ, if desired.
- You may use raisins in place of the cranberries, if desired.

Beautiful Blueberry Tartlets

MAKES 10 TO 12 TARTLETS

Yum is all I can say when describing these petite and perfect little fruit tarts. A whole-grain tortilla provides a crisp and satisfying crust, while fresh, plump blueberries mixed with a bit of maple syrup and cinnamon provide a scrumptious filling.

TARTLETS

- 1 large (10 to 11-inch) whole-grain or whole wheat tortilla
- 1 cup fresh blueberries
- 1 teaspoon whole-grain pastry flour (gluten-free is fine)
- 1¼ teaspoons maple syrup
- ⅛ teaspoon ground cinnamon
- 1½ teaspoons vegan cane sugar

TOPPINGS

- 1½ rounded teaspoons vegan cane sugar, plus more as desired
- 1½ teaspoons maple syrup, plus more as desired

Preheat the oven to 375 degrees F. Put the tortilla on a cutting board and cut the tortilla into 10 to 12 rounds, using a 2½ to 2¾-inch round cookie cutter. Carefully press a tortilla round inside each cup of a 12-cup mini-muffin tin. Repeat with the remaining tortilla rounds, so that each mini-muffin cup is snugly lined with a tortilla round, making 12 cups in all.

Put the blueberries, flour, 1¼ teaspoons maple syrup, ⅛ teaspoon cinnamon and 1½ teaspoons vegan cane sugar into a medium-sized bowl and gently stir with a large spoon until coated. Divide the blueberry mixture evenly among the tortilla "crusts" in the muffin tin. Bake for 14 to 17 minutes, or until the edges of the tortillas are crisp and golden and the blueberry filling is bubbling.

Put the pan on a wire rack. Top each tartlet with a rounded ⅛ teaspoon sugar and about ⅛ teaspoon maple syrup. Let cool 20 minutes. Put the tartlets into the refrigerator and let chill at least 2 hours before serving. Stored covered in the refrigerator, the tartlets will keep for 1 day.

Tasty Little Baked Apples

MAKES 8 SERVINGS

These tasty little gems make a lovely dessert. Have some apples left over? Serve them for breakfast, as they make a delightfully sweet and nutritious morning treat!

- 8 medium Gala or Fiji apples, cored
- ⅓ cup chopped pecans
- ⅓ cup sweetened dried cranberries
- ¼ cup raisins
- 2 tablespoons raw unsalted sunflower seeds
- 2 tablespoons dark brown sugar
- 1 tablespoon maple syrup
- ½ teaspoon ground cinnamon

Preheat the oven to 375 degrees F. Line a 9-inch square baking pan with unbleached parchment paper, leaving a 4-inch overhang on two opposite sides of the pan. Arrange the apples in the pan, making certain they are tightly packed and standing upright.

Put the pecans, cranberries, raisins, sunflower seeds, brown sugar, maple syrup and cinnamon into a medium-sized bowl and stir with a large spoon to combine. Spoon one-eighth of the pecan mixture into each apple, packing it down *very* tightly. Bring the excess parchment paper over the apples and fold to lightly seal. Tent the parchment with foil to tightly seal.

Bake for 45 to 55 minutes, or until the apples are soft, and the filling is bubbling. Cool for 30 minutes before serving, or let stand longer and serve at room temperature. Serve with *Basic Cashew Cream* (page 71) drizzled over the top. Alternately, refrigerate for 4 to 6 hours and serve the apples cold. Covered and stored in the refrigerator, leftover apples will keep for about 2 days.

Festive Sweet Potato Pie

Sweet potato pie adds a festive flourish to the close of any holiday meal. Using pre-baked sweet potatoes and a quick-to-prepare cookie crust makes it easy. This satisfying dessert will truly dazzle your family and guests alike.

CRUST

- 2½ to 3 cups vegan cookie crumbs (I like ginger cookies for this, see note)
- ⅓ (heaping) cup vegan margarine, plus more if needed

FILLING

- 2 to 3 very large (or 4 to 5 small) baked sweet potatoes, cooled (see note)
- ⅓ cup maple syrup
- ¼ teaspoon allspice
- ¼ teaspoon ground ginger
- ¼ teaspoon ground cinnamon

TOPPING

- 1½ tablespoons dark brown sugar
- ½ teaspoon ground cinnamon
- 12 to 16 pecan and/or walnut halves, for garnish

Preheat the oven to 375 degrees F.

Put the cookie crumbs into a medium-sized bowl. Add the vegan margarine and incorporate it into the crumbs using a dough blender or large fork, until combined. Add a bit more margarine if crumbs still seem dry. Press the crust into an un-oiled 9-inch pie plate. Bake for 7 minutes. Put the plate on a wire rack to cool for 10 minutes.

Meanwhile, slice each sweet potato in half lengthwise. Scoop out the pulp, using a teaspoon or grapefruit spoon. Put the pulp into a medium-sized bowl and add the maple syrup, allspice, ginger and cinnamon. Mash well, using a potato masher or large fork, until the mixture is almost smooth. Pour the filling over the crust and smooth the top, using an offset spatula or rubber spatula. Bake for 25 to 27 minutes, or until almost set.

While the pie bakes, put 1½ tablespoons brown sugar and ½ teaspoon ground cinnamon into a small bowl and stir to combine. Remove the pie from the oven. Sprinkle the sugar/cinnamon mixture evenly over the top of the pie, then "swirl" it into the top of the pie using an offset spatula or rubber spatula, making certain all of the sugar/cinnamon mixture is moistened with some of the filling. Bake for 5 to 7 minutes more, or until pie is almost set.

Put the pie on a wire rack and garnish with the pecans and/or walnuts. Let cool 30 minutes, then refrigerate for at least 4 hours before serving. Covered and stored in the refrigerator, leftover pie will keep for about 2 days.

CHEF'S NOTES:

- To make cookie crumbs, put about 3½ to 4 cups of broken up vegan cookies into a blender and process into coarse crumbs.
- Sweet potatoes may be baked up to 48 hours in advance of preparing this recipe. Store tightly covered in the refrigerator until ready to use.

Crazy Coffee Chocolate Mousse

MAKES 8 TO 10 SERVINGS

For adults only, this coffee-laden mousse really has jazzy pizzazz. Rich, creamy and *super* chocolaty, serve this rich offering at the close of any elegant meal and you will receive rave reviews.

- ½ cup nondairy milk

- ¼ cup very strong, cold coffee

- 3 tablespoons maple syrup

- 1 block (14 to 16 ounces) extra-firm regular tofu, drained and broken into chunks

- 1 teaspoon vanilla extract

- 1 cup plus 1 tablespoon 70% cacao vegan dark chocolate chips, plus 8 to 10 more for garnish

Put the nondairy milk, coffee and maple syrup into a small saucepan and bring to a simmer over medium-low heat.

Put the tofu, vanilla and chocolate chips into a blender, in the order listed. Pour the simmering nondairy milk mixture over the tofu and chocolate chips and process for 1 minute, or until very smooth and creamy and no lumps remain. Pour the mixture into 8 to 10 espresso cups or small dessert dishes.

Garnish each with 1 chocolate chip. Refrigerate for at least 6 hours before serving, or until well chilled. Serve cold. Covered and stored in the refrigerator, leftover mousse will keep for about 2 days.

Vanilla Cream-Chocolate Pudding Parfaits

MAKES 6 SERVINGS

Beautiful to look at, lovely to eat, these simple but elegant parfaits will surely please vanilla *and* chocolate lovers alike.

VANILLA CREAM

- ½ block (7 to 8 ounces) extra-firm regular tofu, drained and broken into chunks

- 3 tablespoons maple syrup

- 1 teaspoon vanilla extract

CHOCOLATE PUDDING

- ½ cup nondairy milk

- 3 tablespoons maple syrup

- ½ block (7 to 8 ounces) extra-firm regular tofu, drained and broken into chunks

- 1 teaspoon vanilla extract

- ⅔ cup 55% cacao vegan dark chocolate chips, plus 6 more for garnish

To make the vanilla cream, put all of the vanilla cream ingredients into a blender and process until completely smooth. Transfer the vanilla cream mixture to a medium-sized bowl.

To make the chocolate pudding, put the nondairy milk and maple syrup into a small saucepan and bring to a simmer over medium-low heat. Put the tofu, vanilla and chocolate chips into the blender in the order listed. As soon as the nondairy milk mixture begins to bubble, immediately pour it over the tofu-chocolate chip mixture in the blender. Process for 1 minute, or until completely smooth.

To assemble the parfaits, start with six mini-martini glasses or small parfait glasses. For each serving, spoon about one-sixth of the vanilla cream into the bottom of the glass, then top with about one-sixth of the chocolate pudding, and garnish with a single chocolate chip. Repeat with the remaining glasses to make 6 servings in all. Refrigerate for 6 hours, or until completely chilled, before serving. Covered and stored in the refrigerator, leftover pudding will keep for about 2 days.

White Chocolate Mousse

MAKES 8 SERVINGS

This fabulously fluffy mousse has a not-too-sweet delicate taste and smooth texture that rivals the dairy-laden version. Classic in every way, it makes an excellent finish to an elegant meal, but it's easy to prepare, so it serves well as an afternoon snack or weeknight treat too. (My husband likes to eat it for breakfast!)

- ¾ **cup sweetened vanilla flavored nondairy milk**
- **2 tablespoons maple syrup**
- **1 block (14 to 16 ounces) extra-firm regular tofu, drained and broken into chunks**
- ½ **teaspoon vanilla extract**
- **7 ounces (about 1⅓ cups) vegan white chocolate chips**
- **Mint sprigs (for garnish)**
- **8 raspberries (for garnish)**

Put the nondairy milk and maple syrup into a small saucepan and bring to a simmer over medium-low heat.

Put the tofu, vanilla and white chocolate chips into a blender in the order listed. Pour the simmering nondairy milk over the tofu mixture and process for 30 seconds to 1 minute, or until *completely* smooth. Immediately pour the mousse into eight small dessert dishes, small parfait-style glasses or mini-martini glasses.

Refrigerate for 4 hours, or until completely chilled. Garnish each dessert with a sprig of mint and a raspberry, and serve. Covered and stored in the refrigerator, leftover mousse will keep for about 2 days.

Cherry-Chocolate Pudding Bites

MAKES 36 "BITES"

These fun and fabulous sweet treats feature a baked tortilla base covered in chocolate and filled with a delightful cherry-chocolate pudding. YUM.

BOWLS

- 3 whole wheat tortillas (each 10 to 11-inches in diameter) (see note)
- ¾ cup vegan dark chocolate chips (55% to 70% cacao)
- 1 tablespoon vegan powdered sugar, plus more as needed

PUDDING

- ⅓ cup sweetened nondairy milk
- ¼ cup maple syrup
- 3 heaping tablespoons black cherry or cherry preserves
- ½ block (7 to 8 ounces) extra-firm regular tofu, well drained and broken into chunks
- 1 cup vegan dark chocolate chips (55% to 70% cacao)

Preheat the oven to 350 degrees F. Put 1 tortilla on a cutting board and cut out 12 rounds using a 2¼ to 2½-inch round cookie cutter. Repeat with the remaining tortillas, making 36 rounds in all.

Carefully fit each round into the inside of a cup in each of three 12-cup mini-muffin tins. Repeat with the remaining rounds, so that each mini-muffin cup is snugly lined with a tortilla round, making 36 cups in all (see note).

Bake for 7 minutes, or until the tortilla bowls are almost firm and slightly golden on the bottom and around the edges. Transfer to a wire rack and let cool about 20 minutes.

While the tortilla bowls cool, melt the vegan chocolate chips in a double boiler over medium-low heat. Turn to *very* low and carefully dip the bottom of each tortilla bowl into the melted chocolate, using a small rubber spatula to help spread the melted chocolate over the bottom and make it smooth. Put the chocolate covered bowls upside down on a sheet pan that has been lined with unbleached parchment paper.

Once all of the tortillas have been covered in chocolate, put them in the freezer for 3 to 7 minutes to firm up slightly. Once the chocolate is almost firm, arrange the chocolate covered bowls, *bowl side up*, on a wire rack and dust the insides with powdered sugar. Return the bowls to the parchment-lined sheet pan and refrigerate until the chocolate coating is completely firm.

To make the pudding, heat the nondairy milk and maple syrup in a small saucepan over medium-low heat until simmering.

Put the preserves and tofu into a blender, then add the chocolate chips. Pour in the simmering nondairy milk mixture and process for 45 seconds to 1 minute, or until *completely* smooth.

Spoon about a tablespoon of the mixture into each of the chocolate tortilla bowls, dividing it evenly among the bowls. Cover and refrigerate for 6 to 24 hours. Serve cold. Covered and stored in the refrigerator, leftover bites will keep for about 3 days.

CHEF'S NOTES:
- For a gluten-free option, use your favorite gluten-free tortilla, such as a brown rice tortilla.
- If you do not have three 12-cup mini-muffin tins, you can prepare one tin at a time.

Pecan-Date Truffles

MAKES 9 TRUFFLES

My brother-in-law loves Medjool dates, so I created this recipe when he and my sister came for New Year's Day dinner last year. So easy and deeee-lish!

- 9 large Medjool dates, pitted
- ¼ cup chopped pecans
- 1 tablespoon maple syrup
- 1 to 2 teaspoons vegan powdered sugar

Line a small baking sheet with unbleached parchment paper.

Put the dates, pecans and maple syrup into a high-performance blending appliance and process to the consistency of very soft dough. Transfer the date mixture to a medium-sized bowl. (The dough will be *very* soft and sticky!)

Put the powdered sugar into a small bowl. Scoop out a heaping tablespoon of the date mixture, using a cookie scoop or tablespoon. With your hands, roll it into a ball. *Gently* roll the date-ball in the powdered sugar until coated. Shake off excess sugar and put the date-ball (truffle) on the prepared sheet. Continue in this manner until you have 9 truffles.

Refrigerate for 4 to 6 hours, or overnight. Covered tightly and stored in the refrigerator, leftover truffles will keep for about 3 days.

Chocolate, Almond and Cherry Clusters

MAKES 12 SERVINGS

Crunchy almonds covered in a delectable dark chocolate candy coating and flavored with coconut and dried cherries offer a satisfying indulgence. These chocolaty, nutty snacks will fly off your table, so you may want to prepare a double-batch! (So easy to make, too.) YUM!

- 1¼ cups raw almonds

- ⅓ cup vegan dark chocolate chips (55% to 70% cacao)

- ¼ cup unsweetened shredded dried coconut

- ⅓ cup sweetened or unsweetened dried cherries

Preheat the oven to 400 degrees F. Line a large, rimmed baking sheet with unbleached parchment paper. Line a 12-cup mini-muffin tin with colorful mini cupcake liners.

Spread the almonds in a single layer on the prepared baking sheet. Bake for 5 to 8 minutes, or until hot and slightly golden, stirring often and checking every 2 minutes to prevent burning.

Carefully transfer the almonds to a large, heatproof bowl. Immediately sprinkle the chocolate chips and coconut over the hot almonds, and let stand for 10 to 20 seconds to let the chips begin to melt. Stir with a large spoon until the almonds are evenly coated with the chocolate chips and coconut. Immediately fold in the dried cherries.

Drop a heaping tablespoon of the almond mixture into each of the prepared paper liners. Refrigerate for 1 to 2 hours, or until set. Stored in an airtight container in the refrigerator, the almond clusters will keep for 3 to 5 days.

Peanut Butter-Cranberry-Pecan Fudge Bites

Here's a treat that will surely satisfy your sweet tooth *and* chocolate cravings. This fudgy confection will fit the bill for a rich dessert, but it's full of healthy ingredients, making it a nutritious snack for kids and adults alike.

- ¾ cup smooth peanut butter

- ⅓ cup maple syrup

- 3½ ounces vegan dark chocolate bar, cut into small pieces (candy bar, not baking chocolate)

- ⅓ cup chopped pecans or sunflower seeds

- ¼ cup sweetened dried cranberries (see note)

CHEF'S NOTE: You may use dried cherries or raisins in place of the cranberries, if you prefer.

Lightly coat an 8-inch square baking pan with vegan margarine. Put the peanut butter and maple syrup into a large bowl and briskly stir with a fork until well combined.

Melt the chocolate in a double boiler over low heat. Pour the melted chocolate into the peanut butter mixture and stir until thoroughly combined. Fold in the pecans (or sunflower seeds) and cranberries. Transfer to the prepared pan. Spread in an even layer and smooth the top. Score the surface into 16 to 20 rectangles with a table knife; this will make it easier to cut the fudge after it has set.

Cover with foil and refrigerate for 2 to 4 hours, until firm. Cut into 16 to 20 squares. Serve chilled. Stored in an airtight container in the refrigerator, the fudge will keep for about 2 days.

281

CHAPTER FIFTEEN
Jazzylicious Menu Plans

A well-planned menu makes serving plant-based fare easier and ultimately delicious. Here are a few of my favorite menu combinations to get you started!

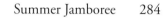

Meal Plans

Summer Jamboree

SALAD
Almost Caesar Salad (page 112)

MAIN COURSE
Tofu-Teriyaki Kebabs (page 186)
Basic Quinoa (page 237)

DESSERT
White Chocolate Mousse (page 275)

Vegan Drive-In

MAIN DISH
Sunny Black Bean Burgers (page 194)

SIDE DISHES
Colorful Coleslaw with a Kick! (page 107)
Russet Oven Fries (page 232) or Colorful
Confetti Fries (page 234)

DESSERT
Better Than Apple Pie (page 254)

New Year's Eve Soirée

SOUP
Cauliflower-Leek Soup with Sweet Paprika
(page 142)

SALAD
Anne's Spicy Arugula Salad (page 121)

MAIN DISH
Gingered Portobello Steaks (page 190)

SIDE DISHES
Pretty Orange Mash Up (page 230)
Roasted Asparagus (page 223)

DESSERT
Crazy Coffee Chocolate Mousse (page 270)

Let's Celebrate!

SOUP

Roasted Carrot and Butternut Squash Soup (page 138)

ENTRÉE

Really Yummy Pecan Sunflower Seed and
Zucchini Loaf (page 196)
Simple Mushroom Gravy (page 76)

SIDE DISHES

Red Potato and Cauliflower Mash (page 230)
Lemon-Sesame Broccoli (page 214)

DESSERT

Pecan-Date Truffles (page 279)

Spring Supper

SALAD
Sweet Arugula Salad (page 108)

ENTRÉE
Asparagus Tart (page 146)

SIDE DISHES
Cashew Stuffed Artichokes (page 216)
Roasted Cauliflower with Red Onion and
Sweet Paprika (page 229)

DESSERT
Beautiful Blueberry Tartlets (page 266)

Wow! Weekend Brunch

SALAD
Almost Ambrosia Salad (page 124)

MAIN DISHES
Fabulous French Toast Bake (page 34)
Mini-Quiche Cups (page 26)

BEVERAGE
Banana-Berry Smoothie (page 40)

DESSERT
Chocolate-Banana Gratin (page 258)

Bollywood-Style

ENTRÉE
Rajma (Hearty Kidney Bean Stew) (page 206)

SIDE DISHES
Turmeric Quinoa (page 237)
Mini-Cauliflower Bites (page 228)

BEVERAGE
Golden Cashew Milk (page 62)

Tex-Mex Menu

SALAD
Tex-Mex Salad Bowl (page 110)

ENTRÉE
Seitan Fajitas with Cashew Sour "Cream"
(page 198)

SIDE DISH
Spicy Rice (page 233)

BEVERAGE or DESSERT
Banana-Mango Smoothie (page 50)

ACKNOWLEDGEMENTS

My deepest gratitude goes out to many people (friends, family and colleagues) for their continued support of my vegan journey! An eternal thank you goes to my loyal husband Andy, whose faith in me (and continued eagerness to be my chief recipe tester) makes all of my hard work come to life.

To my family and friends, I hope you know how much your encouragement has meant to me all these years. You have been my community, my rock, and I have gained so much from your input and love. Thank you to my beautiful, incredible sister Julie and awesome brother-in-law, Rob—without your hard work and support, this season could not have happened!

A big thank you goes to the wonderful Scribe Publishing Company team—for your talent and guidance throughout the process of writing this book. Much appreciation goes to Jennifer Baum whose organizational skills, editing prowess and creative vision brought this book to full fruition. Thank you to Miguel Camacho for the attractive book design and to Inanna Arthen, Mel Corrigan, Judy Filipski-Baum, Chris Lacy and Bill Lacy for proofreading with such patience and caring.

My deepest thanks goes to our incredible guests this season—celebrated jazz singer, Kelle Jolly; Bollywood writer and producer, Sri Rao; and superstar Broadway choreographer and director, Chase Brock—who contributed uplifting music, spirited dance, fascinating fun and lots of life this season! A thank you goes to the cast of *Music Man* for taking part in the show, along with the Flat Rock Playhouse, for allowing us to film segments inside their fantastic theater.

I thank (with *all* my heart)—our industrious, hard working and super-talented *Jazzy Vegetarian* television crew. A giant thank you goes to our incredible Culinary Supervisor, Anne Landry, for her awesome cooking skills and for establishing a great vibe on set while organizing all of the very challenging culinary requirements this season. Thank you (a million times over) to Rob White for his excellent camera work and steadfast help and to Julie Snyder for her ninja sous chef skills, combined with her help as wardrobe coordinator and crew member! Many thanks goes to Tish Christopher for her dedication in the kitchen (doing *whatever* was needed) and for helping us get the food onto the set each episode. Much appreciation to Haley Parrish for making me presentable every day with her extensive talents in both hair and make-up.

292

Thanks to Regina Eisenberg, who has never wavered in her commitment to *Jazzy Vegetarian*, helping to bring the television series from dream to reality. I am indebted to David Davis, Cheri Arbini, Kelsey Wallace and all of our team at *Oregon Public Broadcasting* for giving the *Jazzy Vegetarian* a home on public television, and I gratefully appreciate Gayle Loeber and *NETA* for their excellent job in distributing the program.

Many thanks goes to the awesome *Drayton Mills* team, and especially to Tara Sherbert, for inviting us to film this season in your stunning luxury lofts!

I need to offer a big jazzy thank you to Cheryl Nelson, who worked tirelessly in securing our underwriter for this season. And gratitude goes out to our Season Six underwriter, *Bertolli*, for supporting us to make this season happen!

A heart-filled thanks to my growing network of amazing vegan authors, recipe developers and bloggers—Dianne Wenz, Nava Atlas, Annie Oliverio, Zel Allen, Zsu Dever and so many more—for your continued support through the years.

And to all of the animals on this Earth—as always—this book is for you.

293

ABOUT THE AUTHOR

Laura Theodore is a recognized public television personality, award-winning celebrity vegan chef, radio host, cookbook author and award-winning actor and recording artist. She is one of the foremost leaders in the plant-based food movement and has been creating healthy and delicious plant-based recipes for over twenty years. Laura is the on-camera host of the highly successful, award-winning *Jazzy Vegetarian* plant-based cooking series on public television, as well as the host of the popular podcast radio show, *Jazzy Vegetarian Radio*.

Ms. Theodore is author of *Laura Theodore's Vegan-Ease: An Easy Guide to Enjoying a Plant-Based Diet*, *Jazzy Vegetarian Classics: Vegan Twists on American Family Favorites* and *Jazzy Vegetarian: Lively Vegan Cuisine Made Easy and Delicious*. She is a major contributor to *The China Study All-Star (Recipe) Collection*; and Laura's recipes can also be found in the Amazon number one bestseller, *Living the Farm Sanctuary Life*, by Gene Baur.

Laura is recipient of a "Taste Award" for "Best Health and Fitness Program (Food and Diet)," and in 2016 she was inducted into the *Taste Hall of Fame*. Laura was also honored with a "Special Achievement Taste-Award," along with the likes of Martha Stewart and Emeril Lagasse, and she has been recognized by *VegNews* magazine with a "Totally Tubular Veggie Award." In 2017, Laura was recognized with a "Top 100 Vegetarian Blog Award."

Laura is a featured plant-based culinary expert in the new groundbreaking documentary film, *Food Choices*, released on *Netflix*. In addition, Laura has made guest appearances as a celebrity chef on ABC, NBC, CBS and FOX, *The Talk* on CBS, *Insider/Entertainment Tonight* (HBO Red Carpet), *News 4*-NBC, *Fox News 8*, *The Better Show* (BVN) and the *WCBS Health & Wellbeing Report*. Laura has written food columns for *Mother Earth Living* and she has been featured in the *New York Times*, *New York Daily News*, *VegNews*, *Family Circle*, *Readers Digest*, *PBS Food*, *Naked Food* and *Healthy Aging*, among other highly respected news, food and lifestyle-related journals.

A critically acclaimed singer and songwriter, Laura has recorded six solo CDs, including *Tonight's the Night*, which received a "Musician Magazine Award." Her 2009 CD release with the late, great Joe Beck entitled *Golden Earrings* received a GRAMMY® nod in the category of "Best Jazz Vocal Album." On the acting side of things, Laura has appeared in over sixty plays and musicals, including two years in the Off Broadway hit show *Beehive*, earning her a coveted "Backstage Bistro Award." She was honored with the "Denver Critics Drama Circle Award" as "Best Actress in a Musical" for her starring role as Janis Joplin in the world premiere production of *Love, Janis*.

With her love for good food, compassion for animals and enthusiasm for great music, multi-talented author Laura Theodore truly *is* the *Jazzy Vegetarian*.

INDEX

299

302

Additional Titles
by Laura Theodore

Books

Jazzy Vegetarian: Lively Vegan Cuisine Made Easy and Delicious

Jazzy Vegetarian Classics: Vegan Twists on American Family Favorites

Laura Theodore's Vegan-Ease: An Easy Guide to Enjoying a Plant-Based Diet

To purchase autographed copies of Laura's Cookbooks, DVDs or
CDs, please visit: www.jazzyvegetarian.com

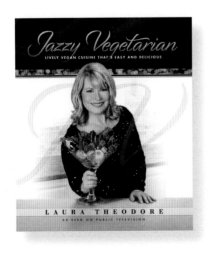
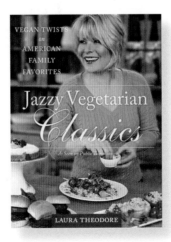

CDs

Golden Earrings (Whaling City Sound)

Tonight's The Night (Bearcat Records)

Live at Vartan Jazz (Vartan Jazz Lable)

What the World Needs Now is Love (Bearcat Records)

Organic Love 100% Natural (Release date, late 2018)

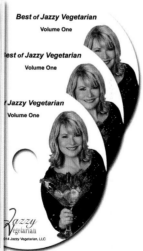

DVD
(3-DVD Set)

The Best Of Jazzy Vegetarian

ONLINE RESOURCES

Where to find Laura Theodore and Jazzy Vegetarian Online

Websites:

www.jazzyvegetarian.com

www.lauratheodore.com

www.vegan-ease.com

Streaming Online Television Channel:

www.jazzyvegetariantv.com

Social Media:

www.twitter.com/Jazzyvegetarian

www.facebook.com/JazzyVegetarian

www.pinterest.com/JazzyVegetarian